The Hundred Yard Dash Man:
New And Selected Poems

Barry Goldensohn

Fomite
Burlington, VT

Poems copyright 2014 © by Barry Goldensohn
Art copyright 2014 © by Douglas Kinsey

All rights reserved. No part of this book may be reproduced in any form or by any means without the prior written consent of the publisher, except in the case of brief quotations used in reviews and certain other noncommercial uses permitted by copyright law.

ISBN-13: 978-1-937677-68-8
Library of Congress Control Number: 2014933607

Fomite
58 Peru Street
Burlington, VT 05401
www.fomitepress.com

Cover Art - Douglas Kinsey

This book is dedicated to my father Joseph Benjamin Goldensohn, 1907-1993, who held records for the hundred yard dash in his time in the New York City high schools and at City College.

I consider the hundred yard dash very like the lyric poem.

Books by Barry Goldensohn

Saint Venus Eve
Uncarving the Block
The Marrano
Dance Music (a chapbook)
East Long Pond, with Lorrie Goldensohn (a chapbook)
The Listener Aspires to the Condition of Music

Acknowledgements

Agenda (London): Pieces for the Suicide of Paul Celan
AGNI: Bathsheba, Fugitive Night Song, Religion of Art Revisited
Arion's Dolphin: Three Ring Circus
Harvard Review: Thelonious Monk Dancing
Hunger Mountain: The Swan and Leda, Managed Grief,
New Republic: Remains, The String Quartet
New York Review of Books: The Hundred Yard Dash Man, Back Roads, Driving Westward to San Diego
Notre Dame Review: Deep Lake (a section of Immersion)
Poetry: Aphrodites, The Louvre, Point Lobos, Before Beethoven's Creation of Music as Personal Expression, The Arch of Titus, The Toy, On a Portrait of Thomas Wyatt, Morning of Execution, Time and the String Quartet Domesticate Eros, The Alert Scribe, Noli me tangere, Flaubert and Emma Bovary, War and Peace, The Listener Aspires to the Condition of Music
Prairie Schooner: Nomos, Logos
Rune (University of Toronto): Uncarving the Block
Salmagundi: Dance, Ignorance, The Forerunners, To Hollis Frampton, The Summer I Spent Screwing in the Back Seat of Station Wagons, National Portrait Gallery, Bottoming Out, Immersion, Dance Music, Rediscovering Wonder, Rest, Mater Dolorosa, The Bat, My Gallery, In Mexico, The Entitled, Subway, Last Act: Don Giovanni, Tarzan and Co., Margaret Roper
Slate.com: April 26, 1937, Repeats, The Natural, Toad Skin, Reading Faust when Young, The Natural, Mountain Lion
Suss: A Treatise on Ungovernment, Learning from Nature
The Yale Review: She Tiresias, Lao Tzu Rebuked, Leaving the Body
The Hardy Review, The Swan and Leda, The Pitcher, At the Frick, Counting

Immersion appeared in *East Long Pond* and the poem Dance Music appeared in *Dance Music,* chapbooks published by Cummington Press

The Arch of Titus appeared in *The Poetry Anthology, 1912-2002: Ninety Years of America's Most Distinguished Verse Magazine*

The Bat, Lao Tzu Rebuked, The Summer I Spent Screwing in the Back Seats of Station Wagons, Rest, appeared in *Poets of the New Century*

Thelonious Monk Dancing, Burmese Temple Bell, The Listener Aspires to the Condition of Music, David and Saul, Carmens, Last Act: Don Giovanni, Time and the String Quartet Domesticate Eros, What is the Condition of Music, Padre Antonio Vivaldi, The String Quartet, appeared in *The Listener Aspires to the Condition of Music*

Contents

I

The Hundred Yard Dash Man	3
The Summer I Spent Screwing in the Back Seats of Station Wagons	4
Marriage Vows, 1956	5
In Mexico	6
Back Roads	7
Losing Boundaries	8
Rediscovering Wonder: Santa Cruz Mts, California, 1989	9
Before Beethoven's Creation of Music as Personal Expression	11
April 26, 2006	12
War and Peace	13
Walking in Fog	15
The Coast	16

II

Thelonius Monk Dancing	21
Reading Faust when Young	23
A Night at the Theater	24
National Portrait Gallery, London	25
Aphrodites, The Louvre	26
To Hollis Frampton	27
She, Tiresias	28
Mater Dolorosa	29
Richard II: the religion of art	30
Burmese Temple Bell	31
Dance	32

Lao Tzu Rebuked	33
Rest	34
Arch of Titus	36
Machine for Bringing on the Second Coming	37
The Quilt of Aphrodite	39
The Swan and Leda	41
A UNE PASSANTE, Fifth Avenue Variation	42
Bottoming Out	43

III

The Statue	47
Forbidden Games: at the Berlin Holocaust Memorial	48
A Wedding	49
Wooden Crucifix 15th Century	50
The Natural, Brooklyn, 1950	51
Haystack	52
My Gallery	53
The Forerunners	55
Remains	56

IV

Subway	59
Driving Westward to San Diego	60
Point Lobos	61
A Treatise on Ungovernment	63
Memorial	66
Managed Grief	67
Obit	68
Old Home Day	69
Sweet Town	70
The Gossips	71
Leaving the Body	72

Repeats	73
Fugitive's Night Song	74
David And Saul	75

V

Pieces for the Suicide of Paul Celan	79
At the Frick	82
The Execution of Lady Jane Grey	83
Ignorance	84
Carmens, the Audition	85
From *The Book Of Blessings*	86
The Entitled	87
Toad Skin	88
Mountain Lion	89
Learning from Nature	91
Meditations on Violence	92

From Saint Venus Eve (1972)

The Listener Aspires to the Condition Of Music	103
Flaubert and Emma Bovary	104
Noli me tangere	*105*
Nomos, Logos	106
On Meeting the Blessed Virgin Jane Austen	108
Padre Antonio Vivaldi	109
Secret Love Song	110
Speech on the Telephone	111
The Crow Down Comforter	112
Paolo and Francesca	113
The Judges	114
The Scribe	116

From Uncarving The Block

Uncarving the Block	121
Epithalamium	130
Antethalamium	132
Burying a Child (R.B. 1969-1974)	133
Famous Lovers	134
Last Act: Don Giovanni	135
Our Other Mind Problem	137
The Morning of Execution	140
The Old Prince	141
The Revolution Decides Not to Occur	142
Three Ring Circus	143
Time and the String Quartet Domesticate Eros	144
Tired with The Hunt and Cold	145
What *Is* the Condition of Music?	146

From The Marrano (1988)

The Kabalist	149
The Marrano	150
A Librarian of Alexandria	151
A Short Season in Hell	153
After the Revolution	155
Coney Island Roller Coaster	156
Family Plot	157
Great Horned Owl	158
Margaret Roper	159
Poem Beginning With a Line by Hollis Frampton	162
Puppet Theater	164
Tarzan & Co.	165
The Drawing of Thomas Wyatt by Holbein	167
The Dybbuk	168

The Religion Of Art: 1 Feb 58	169
The String Quartet	171
The Toy	172
The *Via Negativa*, Ojai, California	174
For Hollis Frampton (d. 1984)	175
U.S. Signal Corps Footage	177
To all The Gods at Once: A Prayer for Mercy	178

Dance Music 183

from East Long Pond

Immersion	193

I

The Hundred Yard Dash Man

I carried him lightly,
eighty pounds, my height,
half my weight
with enough body sense—
the old track star—
to work in my arms to balance
his remaining mass
as easy live weight.
It became his last voyage,
from living room to bed—
this carrying was comfort to both.
Morphine had ended months
of pain—genial now,
euphoric, enjoying himself,
with his daughter, and me, his son.
"You must have gotten stronger,"
he said, dismissing the loss
of body with a joke.
He knew he was on his way
out the door, and was easy
though less clear for me
as I laid him down in bed
and laid myself in the twin
cold, rumpled, sour.
When hushed voices woke me
saying "He died last night,"
I couldn't open my eyes
and lay there frozen
among the murmuring women.
He had slipped silently
through the black door
he left open for me.

The Summer I Spent Screwing In The Back Seats Of Station Wagons

was the last summer that lasted all summer.
This was not—do not misread the title—
screwing the seats in, but climbing in
the back and screwing as fast as I could.
It was always the same, open the back and fling
in the power driver and the big tool
box with the braces and screws as the tall Pole
pressed the window firmly into place,
as I would drill the holes, line up the clamps,
and screw them in. If the clamps sat too tight
the window cracked and then a flurry of work
as we swarmed ahead of our spot on the line,
the tall Pole and I at Fisher Bodies
in Euclid, Ohio, and rushed to return to our place.
I kept bashing my hands and my nights were crushed,
and in all that soul exhausting work
the cars were as rotten as we could make them.
There was nothing of ourselves we wanted to see
in what we did to Chevy Kingswood and Nomad
and Pontiac Safari with pubescent tailfins.
This was in Euclid, who looked on Beauty bare,
Ohio, whose three long syllables danced
in only four letters, pronounced ah-hah,
by my fellow workers who wrenched, torqued, and screwed
on the assembly line with me in Euclid, Ohio.
At the end of the day all we had was numbers,
corporate totals. It brought to mind
the boast of Wilt the Stilt that he had fucked
twenty thousand women in his time,
and never, never, the same woman twice.
And as we looked, wearied, at our line of cars
we wondered, how could he tell?

Marriage Vows, 1956

We were claimed by our time, elected
study over prayer, not invulnerable
to the charm of the sacred, of ritual,
even of ceremony when talk of god
was left out. We were married
by a rabbi I revered, who took our youth
and levity as serious, rightly.
After we spoke our dignified vows
and I smashed a glass under foot
the rabbi yoked us by the powers
granted to him by the Laws
of Moses (in Leviticus), of Israel
(meaning the mystical body of the Jewish people,
not the divided, embattled nation of the Middle East
that clamored for our faith with the Freud
-and-Marx dream of the kibbutz) and the State
of New York (meaning where we were born,
whose rich Diaspora culture we loved—
little theaters, coffee shops, and talk, talk, talk—
and where we lived with unforced loyalty.)

In Mexico

The priest, hands soaked by the milk swollen breasts
of the young mother,
grows dizzy with pleasure in his middle age,
reaching under
her embroidered linen blouse,
wide for nursing,
and knows her man could kill him for this
confusing tenderness—
not lust but the recollection of lust
mostly forgotten,
the boyish wonder of a virgin.
How harmonious
the love of his vocation with the love of this woman
but he won't stagger
down the ladder of love and tumble
to his death.
The woman caressed is surprised, mostly
amused and flattered
and fortunately discreet. She likes this priest,
sees him retreat
as his hands fall back to his knees.

Back Roads

After a brief violent storm toppled trees,
deep rooted ones, splayed crowns
across the roads, root balls,
the buried double of the crowns
pulled up as walls of loam in air,
and young ones blown down too,
I drove out to meet my wife and found
most roads blocked, but I knew
the country threeway and fourway roads
like the veins on the back of my hands,
rivers on a map, and I found my way
by zigzag and backtrack till I arrived.

As a child I stared at my father's hands
in fascination at his bulging veins.
With trivial variations this design
is the common one—rivers that join
at the wrist and tangle up the forearm.
That I can tell my own from anyone's
is the clinging illusion of uniqueness
given the superior child, the first son,
the golden son. I still navigate by this.

Losing Boundaries

Looking out to sea from a high bluff
over scrub and beach grass and the unquiet shore
to deep water and the distant mist and clouds
there is no boundary between ocean and sky
even at sunset when the clouds take on the whole
family of reds, pink to maroon, opaque or wispy,
passionate, diffuse, brilliant, shaded
with deep gray or with an incandescence
that fills the whole visible world—you, the grass
we stand on while we breathe in light
my arms around you are no longer mine
but part of you dizzying without boundary
arms, breasts, shoulders, face, your breath in me.

Rediscovering Wonder: Santa Cruz Mts, California, 1989

Slower, and no longer possessing the eyes
of the boyish lover who floated and dove
through these hills engraving them in mind
and in my first camera, a small point-and-shoot thing,
who tried to hold this world by grabbing, snatching,
with the body's faith in that sudden spurt of vision.

Now the unwieldy mounting on a tripod,
composing slowly on the ground glass
of an old view camera, no more fast work
but to see the great curves, delicate ferns
in the deep shadow and each tree precisely,
backlit by fog and set free of background,
clear in the air of its proper distance,
not leaf masses only and the mess of green.
Now the meditative timeless play
with light and the discrimination of planes,
the sodden leaf clinging to pebbles in a clear pool,
and another leaf floating on its surface
along with bright dust and the sky quivering
in ripples through the reflected trees
and trees' shadows.
                      Now to walk with eyes open
and keep them open, not drift inward
with the strong tide that pulls and pulls.

I climbed for the wide view of the slope to the sea,
its lines voluptuous, fragmented, with the faint gold
wash of ripe grass that waves over the deep green,
and set the camera up to stop the passionate
advance of the hills' curves on one another
as the hill above had raised its bulk
over the lower, nearer hill that lay
like the back and buttocks of someone at hand.

And the steep hills no longer plunged and dove
around me (how else could I see
but by stopping to compose with slow control,
when the world races in a dream of one green passionate
fertile surface covering everything?)
the whole body lying naked and open
beneath me inviting wonder with a fierce buzz
at every move I made that seemed to come
from my own ears—no cars, no planes—just me
breathless from climbing. "My heart! my heart!" I thought
but it was not inside me and I saw a nervous cloud
of flies rise in alarm from their platter of fresh dung
whose rich odor encompassed us all.
A red-tailed hawk swung above me and I turned
the camera to the cliff's edge to wait
till he dove to the place he belonged in the design,
before the warm body of the land and the glare
of the sea.
   This patience with the world,
the black draped seclusion as light gathers
on ground glass, sky below, hills
with each intricate tree and the sea above—
easing into focus as the back and lens
tilt and swing and the blue-eyed grass comes clear,
then the dolphin's back as it sinks for air into light,
as the loved body rises from her depths in my mind,
and enters the world to be seen with open eyes
who could so easily blind me with her touch.

Before Beethoven's Creation Of Music As Personal Expression
-a vigil for Lorrie

At her bedside all day and she unconscious—
tubes in, tubes out, tape and bruises,
clamps, catheters to the heart, something
breathing for her, monitors murmuring, knowing
that nothing was yet out of control of the doctors.

And then home and music and collapse
and Beethoven's Quartet in G,
very classical, impersonal,
before his revolution made everything
Beethoven! Beethoven! and my outstretched nerves
the strings they played sweet repetitive
symmetrical structures on—clear, small surprises
that carried me away from myself into myself.

Nothing was yet out of control of the doctors,
the team, their exquisite machines for reading the heart,
breathing for her, monitors murmuring, knowing
this is a vigil I did not keep for my mother,
years ago, she also unconscious,
and neither woman knew whether I kept it or not.

April 26, 2006

This is the day I reach 69,
the elegant union of head to tail, tail to head,
the lover's number, the yin-yang sign,
a celebration of three, the mystic numbers
to guide us through the forbidden grove (now allowed)
to the freely disregarded former god
who was absent from any supervisory role
in the century in which I've lived most of my years
on an orderly, ritual-loving continent,
with well regulated trash collection,
public gardens, smooth lawns, milk
delivered at dawn in cold bottles, clinking and sweating—

screaming and glistening with blood
at the hour of my birth Guernica was carpet bombed
as practice for the time of saturation—
the aghast face through the window that sees
the broken bodies by the light of a bare bulb—
devastating cities thick with targets, human
and other items of civil life: school,
public sculpture in parks, music pavilion, musician,
library, literary life, the writer.

War And Peace
(from the memoirs of a Jewish officer in the Czar's army)

I was a scout and messenger. A shell
burst and I lost my horse, my gun, and woke
sunk in thick alders that bent underneath me
like a soft couch—unhurt, but nearly choked
by the strap of the leather pouch around my throat.
I crawled into the dusk, losing all
boyhood faster than I could grasp
in the silence and stinging fog
of the bombed woods. Half the oaks
with their first small spring leaves
burst and burned like a dead city. I found
the path that led to a spot on the river
too swift to cross on foot. Our cavalry
appeared with an old lieutenant who had turned
their rout into an orderly retreat.

He hung back, dismounted, and we talked
about the tasks we were assigned,
while high on their horses the troop filed across.
Nearing dark, a mist rose from the river.
His face, immobile, shone in the cold
like oiled jade—slabs of soft stone
you could mark with your fingernail;
flat cheeks, a broad nose and high forehead.
I was one of the chosen people—could not fail
my mission and thought of this only, he
of something else that I have struggled since then
to grasp. Was he one of the *lamed vov*,
the holy ones disguised, even from themselves,
scattered through the world who save us with wonders?

His horse had wandered off. He whistled
and it charged up from the river, dumb and eager.

A Golem. Could he have called up two that way?
He gave me the horse and I protested faintly.
Then he ordered me. I stopped my protest.
I was young and full of urgency
with front line messages that bore
on the success of war. He was firm,
that was all, and he leaned back on a hummock
of tall grass as I mounted and plunged through
the river, came up dry on the other side,
and galloped after the troops but kept him with me
as I reenact that ending, carrying both,
two horses, or two on one horse,
or me, or him, flying above the river
with a breast stroke through the air.

I accepted this order without question
as something due in the proper conduct of war
and great affairs. Now he buries himself
inside me, the city of the dead endowing
the city of the living with its gods.

Walking In Fog

Everything looms at me. Hounds tongue
with wet doggy leaves and blue flowers
starts up from the mist streaked hillside.
Standing by itself, framed in fog
the live oak twists black arms above me.
The canyon and the next hill disappear.

An owl on a low branch sits in its silhouette
in the white flame of a wild cherry
and a tiny wren weaves through the sagebrush,
singing as it stops then flashes back in.

Plunging into puffs and gusts of fog
along the road a dying friend wheels
and lunges from cliff wall to cliff edge
in a bright yellow blouse and blue jeans
joyous with losing herself and coming back
in daily magic, you see me then you don't.

The Coast

    Low tide, clear sky,
            a rock dome in the sea,
    shelves of granite
            like a royal stair
    and a mile from shore
            she dragged her kayak
    onto a bed of seaweed,
            peeled off her swimsuit
    and life vest, stowed them
            and climbed the dome
    to sunbathe and sleep.
            She woke to the tide
    rising to drown her.
            The kayak below
    lifted from its kelp bed
            and carried away
    with her gear, she computed
            an hour of air
    with a struggle to swim
            in the irresistible tide
    as the water rose
            on the dome, leisurely,
    in no hurry to end her,
            an hour to detach
    her parents, husband
            infant daughter—
    will he feed her and dress her?
            no matter, he will
    and her terror lacked
            any doubt she will die
    detached from her loves,
            so she closed her eyes
    as the tide climbed her body
            till a great noise—

a copter battering,
        dropping a basket
for her to crawl into
        and enter its belly
naked, ashamed
        of her naked body
to be delivered newborn
        in silver mylar.

II

Thelonius Monk Dancing

What might this figure of great force do?
Or not do? Seeming uncontrolled he hit
and poked at the piano without error
then rose and wandered off around the floor

doing a march time heavy footed non-dance
dance, slow turns, clown twirls, arm flaps, he cowed
us, massive, dazed and full of drunk
menace and disdain for the college crowd

at the Five Spot. His deep control relaxed
and grew perilous, crazy, a wounded bear
mugging at the dates of pretty girls. I
was confused and frightened for him and for

myself—what humiliation would I be called
to witness or undergo, what fall or fight,
with this genius drinking himself to greater
distance, building distraction or rage—how could

any of us tell? The waiters kept his whiskey glass
on the piano filled, fuelling the veering
circuit that ignored then threatened then
disdained to destroy us out of love

for something more important than ourselves.
Helpless, polite, white, we disappeared
behind his music, Ray Copeland's horn
singing brought him round, the drums calmed him

and recalled him to play the piece that had run
through so many variations on the vibes,
sax, horn and drums that only one who could take
a phrase in four directions at once could make it end

as music. He steered his mocking shuffle back to the piano
and his feet danced and his fast gunfighter's hands
on the keys, played and not played, turned the room—
terrorized, confused—into his rich, perilous music.

Reading Faust When Young
for David Mamet

I remember only the leap from the bridge
into the turbulent river after knowledge,
but not what special knowledge or what power
ever came his way in the old story.
I was young when I read it. Immortality
meant art and Faustus was not an artist.
And as for girls, you didn't need the devil,
when you offered everything. What did he really
need to know? Something about the girl—
what she felt and could never say because
she had no words for it? He had little
to say to the Greats. Helen was a peep-show.
And the stuff about his soul—
well, that was religious and historical.

Overreaching for me was natural. I wanted
to know everything, to stay forever in school
taking courses. God and the devil
never figured in. With his snaky tail
the devil was too fanciful to explain
the lines waiting for gas or a bullet and ditch
and fire bombs and carpet bombs and the icy
rapture of ideologues shouting about who to kill
and who to save. My fellow humans were real:
their evil was sufficient. The sacred
was love and art and the political dream.
The world-drunk heart was what I took for the soul,
which dulled the edge of Faustus' sacrifice
and god was never real enough to love or lose.

A Night At The Theater

Hamlet has bored himself into deep (deeper
than you thought you'd ever see on stage) shit,
and glares out at the glassy-eyed audience
and sees, in red lights, EXIT, EXIT, EXIT.

National Portrait Gallery, London

Among the stuffed royals, great minds
disguised in public faces, theirs or not:
Shakespeare pictured as the painter's son;
Donne sedated, copied from a copy;
Newton with a bland, dazed smile; tame
genial Swift, unable to disturb
a Minister; Rochester as himself,
outrageous; Nell Gwyn's rouged nipples;
Locke with heartburn; Byron as phallus errant,
glorious, fake; Blake as glacial statesman;
Auden boiled; Eliot born to bronze,
the escape from personality abandoned;
(I freeze in front of cameras then hate
the frozen face) Holbein, even he,
painted men secure in their own masks;
and the complete public poet, set to instruct
the world in his time, painted by a friend,
forehead high, mouth imploring, eyes
intelligent and full of pain
with the first private face in this house of faces,
Pope, even in death, correcting the nation.

And then I encountered a face I know, still
knowable here, Seamus Heaney,
the arrow of his raised knee aimed
at a window daubed with sun, and his head
held back, leans to the darkened corner,
rapt by something he and the painter withhold,
on display as himself averted, protecting, like all
the faces the public owns, the private life.

Aphrodites, The Louvre

Antiquities: marble floors and walls,
copies of lost bronzes, Aphrodites,
anonymous or by Praxiteles
once or many times removed, preside
with their calm sexuality
flagrant and serene. And the public
faces of the Japanese women
who cluster around the Aphrodites
are masks we know from paintings, woodcuts—
small, red, deeply cut mouths
tightly poised, and downcast eyes, until,
responding to a gesture or a word their faces
open with complex smiles, knowing, eager
to please as they rush to companions saying
one thing with their eyes, another with the set
of their mouths, laughing, ironic, aware.
And the passionate curves of breast, buttock, thigh,
are here calmed by marble and we call them gods
to keep them distant so we can find
some pleasure, some delight, some consolation,
in our defections from their perfect form
like the irregular features and alert,
intelligent air of the woman needing
to cross a wide, dangerous street who might
also consider you with that look that hovers between
confusion and a breathless, calculating urgency.

To Hollis Frampton
(1936-1984)

Breaking out of long wordlessness,
Pound lugged his blood red portable
one sun-white morning in Rapallo
to a table in the garden and typed all day.
Behind the blinds in the dim house
the family stared and whispered.
He addressed a handful of envelopes,
puttered through the rooms for stamps,
and walked, enfeebled but erect,
into town and mailed them. He had spoken
hardly a single word to anyone except
the stoned Allen Ginsberg in ten years.

The letters trickled back from the long dead
friends in distant cities: London—Eliot
and Wyndham Lewis, Ketchum—Hemingway,
Paris—James Joyce, Dublin—Yeats,
and Ford Madox Ford and others I forget.
I said to you, who heard this story
from the family, "A letter
to a dead friend is an art form."
"But you don't mail them," you said,
so I don't.

She, Tiresias

    The snakes disentangled and sliced through the whispering
        grasses.
    When I reached out my hand the rings fell off.

    Unaccustomed masses of my body. Unaccustomed motions.

    I have entered a woman's body as myself
    and someone else: a man
    discovering himself a woman, a woman
    remembering herself a man.

    Constrained by gentle breeding and discretion
    a man of my class does not take. He is given
    and suddenly I can give, and by giving, take. *Dere hart,*
    I say, *how like you this?*

    That boy whipping his head around to look.

    This red dress—the way it sweeps the floor
    will reveal me utterly and confess
    to my abandon, to my gravity.

    No longer moving outside my body
    for pleasure, it flows now from inside,
    stays inside, suffuses, like hunger
    satisfied, and the child I carry
    reconnects me to the world I had been studying
    to leave after the deaths: my young friends
    speared at my side in battle filling my arms with their blood,
    my parents dying in great age. The man
    remaining within me remains astonished.
    This child invisible within me,
    frightens him less and less, who now
    is satisfied not to see with his own eyes.

MATER DOLOROSA

She remembers with stare and sigh
her small face between
her mother's breasts, the twin
scrolls of the law naked,
sunk in the break of them,
milky, round, perfumed,
bathing her cheeks and lips,
exploding sweets in her mouth

as if it were still her mother's
warmth of body that warmed her
after she was divided
as love and law divide,
and came to know herself only
against the bodies of others.

RICHARD II: the religion of art

When in the synagogue last
I was past thirty. My father
was younger by ten years
than the old men weaving in prayer.

We went to pray as we could
for my mother's buried soul.
She had died the week before,
but neither of us could recall

the prayers for the dead
and our sorrow was unconsoled.
The gabble and nodding and groans
tasted alien and cold.

And then in a tiny theater
at Richard the Second a girl
at my elbow coiled to hold back
her sobs but the knot of restraint

unwound at the queen's sorrows,
old, mumbling her words,
the king (played by a woman)
unconcerned, off guard

and my heart knew where sorrow
could find the faith to tear
open its long clenched throat
and sing out its prayer of tears.

Burmese Temple Bell

Each dawn this great bell
is struck for each sin
one hundred eight blows:
the world is gathered in
the circle of its voice
and everywhere within
a great order rung.
It tolls through the school
where sleepy children learn
the ciphers and the rule
to wear inside the face
not rule but sub-rule
that they can never break.
They chant in unison,
breathe in its metal breath,
their cheeks to its brass skin.
My own careless life
summoned by this bell
with its low resonance,
from dreaming half awake
or dawdling with words in a room,
would lose the small self,
the small waste of time
in that trembling embrace and dance
that calls me whole to home.

Dance

this empty stage
an ocean   Deborah Hay

Things grow in it, not on it. No grass, no trees
bending and waving as it moves. It rises and falls
like the chest of a breathing animal. To swim in it
is to immerse in its power, either to fight it
if that is the word for thrashing and kicking across
its unfeeling surface, or to ride on it, gliding and stroking,
to let it carry you, consenting to its direction.
Even when violent storms whip its surface
like water shaken in a jar, only a short way down
and further down, its enormous heart beats calmly,
its breaths are even and deep and the art
of only one dancer is needed to cram
within this stage the perilous ocean undiminished.

Lao Tzu Rebuked

When Lao Tzu warns against the fetishism of commodities
He means to warn us against the false desires
Aroused by fancy food, cars, wine, fancy women, watches,
    men, trophy people
Aroused by women with bodies who must therefore cover
    themselves to their toes
And walk without making noise and forswear white socks
(Women without bodies may swim naked through the air),

Aroused by men muscled like ex-cons in tank tops,
    swaggering,
Inarticulate with sincerity, bold, tender,
By slender, doe-eyed, articulate pattern-weavers
(Men without bodies may swim naked through the air),

About which a Jewish divine remarked, that the scheme
Of satisfying our needs by lopping off our desires
Is like cutting off our feet when we need shoes,
Signifying that the revolution in desire will not occur among
    the Jews.

Rest

There were real ducks in the pond arched
by willows and even the Quakers
tolerated music in the service
(it seemed like pure lament and not
a brash display to false gods)
and I had an intense nostalgia
for the self deceiving dream order,
promises, prayers, gifts, bribes,
and all flesh will come to thee,
and all come home and home-free-all
as we gathered in the light around
the casket of this slight young
woman—beautiful even dead.
Her hair combed straight, she always
seemed a veiled Botticelli,
now with eyelids strictly closed.
From the sexual center cancer everywhere
closed her lungs though she lay very still
in the last days and tried to live
without breathing. Now her real
body remains with a cross in her hands
that beckons upward to the grand design.
And they sang Mozart's *Requiem* that begins
and ends with a prayer for *them,* the dead,
who need eternal rest, perpetual light,
the soul that pleads in terror for mercy
from the judgment at the world's end
that frightens even the just and the virgins.
Salva me, fons pietatis,
fountain of pity, save me.
We learned enough of dread in hope,
even thinking she beat it, that vital
body beat it. There was comfort
in remission for weeks that seemed

perpetual light. Now the cry
of terror takes on ritual fullness,
Salva me...non me perdas...
with music we wished her eternal rest
in the arms of her torturer and killer.
And for our grieving all these voices
in the large musical structure sufficed:
it wasn't overwrought, and the prayer,
not abject, loose talk
about the soul. For all the show
of theatrical emotion, there
was dignity and no shame
in this fear. It is the way, lost,
we want ourselves spoken of, sung of.

Arch Of Titus

　　Disregarding the curse
　　that god will remove your name
　　from the list of the Chosen People
　　for passing through this arch,
　　families of tourists,
　　People Not Chosen,
　　pass through blithely
　　as blithely conquering Romans
　　in the all-encircling frieze
　　destroy the Second Temple
　　and carry away their prize,
　　menorah and chained slaves
　　as beautiful as themselves.

　　Though I've no god to lose
　　nor community of Jews
　　and never shared the need
　　for community of faith
　　I will not stray through
　　in my usual careless way
　　and deny what I have lost.

Machine For Bringing On The Second Coming

With his buttocks gleaming in the open
door way, mooning the street,
Rube Goldberg himself
began the chain thrashing
away inside a girl
on all fours who's focused
on the artful application
of her mouth to the erect
eager apparatus
of a man upon whose face
and in whose mouth
the hungry nether lips
of a tall girl spread
devotedly while her mouth
works away on the next
person in the chain
of alternating sexes
or variously girl
on girl or boy on boy
that extends from the front hall
into the living room
up and over the overstuffed
couch and down the chill
hall to the bathtub, hot
and gurgling, up the stairs,
through bedrooms, on beds
and floors, up the attic stairs,
the tall, the short, blonde
and brown and black, across
the attic to the last ecstatic,
half out the window,
strewing fluffy gouts
of pink insulation,
above the crowd on the lawn

who hear her small cries.
Then she screams
and in her flood clamps her legs
around the head of the man
who also floods as she
begins the wave that lifts
the whole chain.

Like a Tibetan prayer wheel
that completes its infinite
rumble of *om mani padme hum,*
the jewel and the lotus,
whereby the world comes
to its long joyous end,
the ascending moan rouses
the goddess of love from her long
sleep in the arms of war
and our vile, violent species
is drenched in love at last
when she comes through the skies again.

The Quilt Of Aphrodite
a token for Hymen

She made a quilt to cover many lovers
since time for her is infinite and meaningless
and she has countless devotees. She stitched,
embroidered, wove—her methods are impulsive.
She was wild when young and stays young.

Acolytes along the edge, begin
with hunger for adventure like the young
charmer who could choose kings or bankers
but beds her boy under the boardwalk in sand
littered with condoms—Coney Island Jellyfish
in fragrant decay. She is surrounded
by groupies with their hair embroidered
with imitation gold thread, standing in lines
as the players leave the locker room
and each offers herself and is accepted.
We see one nearby on a motel bed
with her sturdy ecstatic limbs just visible
under an enormous left tackle
taking the explosion of a star in her inward dark
and she sings out "I'm so good." And her large man
in the shower says to himself "I'm so good."
And in the back seats of a string of parked cars
around the edge of the endless quilt the hungry
and adventurous are celebrated in intricate
and ingenious positions: the fig tree,
the half rolling hitch, the figure eight.

On the next inward line is the dense crowd
of young students with hands locked swaying
into one another as they walk, restraint
imposed by the public moment straining their bodies
against their unnecessary clothes. The madness

is wild in them without love potions or extravagant vows.
Their limbs are countless and the campus throbs
    across a continent of quilt.

On the next ring toward the center are the harvesters
warm after work, cutting, stacking and bringing in
the August hay to the loft of the great barn
and they rinse away the chaff in the cool river
and lie in pairs atop the sweet hay
in one another's welcoming bodies, tired
after labor (but never too tired)
and the strong thighs part to relieve the great
hunger bred by working near one another
in the heat, cutting, lifting and tossing as one,
satisfied by the chosen man of the day
or the year or the lifelong.

Next are the brides, some in white and lace
and some not bothering, parading before
their families, teary or bored, while the winged son
of Aphrodite, Hymen, sings his wedding song
and his brother Priapus attends the grooms.
Toward the square center lie the young wives
who cannot sleep without the rites of Aphrodite
and in the center the old wives sustain
the extreme adventurous vow whose deep hunger
has not yet abandoned them.

The Swan And Leda

She stares with an infant's adoration
at an unsuspecting male, vain enough
to think he has deserved the gift
of her goggle-eyed, goggle-mouthed attention.
Is she Sincere? Yes! Yes! Authentic?
Yes! She has no idea where she learned
to manage this harpoon aimed at the heart.
Harpoon? No! A noose? No!
                              The trick
is to keep him virile and fully intact to serve
the carnal ache, the life career, to nurture
and swell a tribe. You must envy this oaf
his goofy smile, his eagerness for capture.
The hand inching across the table is intimate. The intent,
the force, the means, entirely indifferent.

A *Une Passante*, Fifth Avenue Variation
an appropriation of Baudelaire

A deafening clutch of diesel buses and a woman
mourning in black brocade with the look
of one who is looked at and knows it, a member
of the painted class, the bread and caviar
of artist and sculptor, swung the hem of her gown
so that her legs, supple marble, flashed
with deliberate carelessness, her eyes
were clear skies breeding storms—
sweetness that thrills, pleasure that kills.

I went delirious. She entered a tall door
past a doorman who would shoot if I tried to follow.
In that moment I was reborn to adore and lose
you who vanished, and I moved on too—
oh I would have loved you and you knew it.

Bottoming Out

After the curtain and the flurry
of hug, snub, gush,
and the sharp snarl of velcro,
he slides his bulk from the cluster
of all the beautiful ones,
removes the tufts of hair,
his galluses, sabots,
the rubber, warty nose
that left his own to flame
in the air of his undressing-
redressing room, fighting
to make real in his mind
the body that was not his body
bathing in Titania,
a caress of warm air,
as if he were really there
in memory, not a dream,
from a fresh time before,
and not a barrel of actor
closing his long career
by rolling among the leapers
who are graceful in waist and limb
and who stroke him and titter and kiss
this lieutenant of the nothing
with nothing to laugh at but loss.

III

The Statue

    Poor Berthold Brecht is now bronze
and sits on a bronze bench now black
outside the Berliner Ensemble. Twice
life size, his knees where children have climbed,
gleam, also where they have stepped, his toes.
There's room to his left on the bench where others sat
that also gleams. In these new times,
the Berlin Wall down, his State kaput,
he would not like to sit near those to his left,
gleaming. His stare is inward and he smiles
like a smug Buddha who has forgiven
the disaster of his consent.

    He is dishonored. His great poems were not
written by this bronze giant. Inscribed
around his seat is his poem "Questions of the Worker-
Reader." The rhetorical questions
insult the worker's intelligence—
a party line poem, and the party's over.
Every morning he is buried in heavy mist
that rises from the river Spree.

Forbidden Games: at the Berlin Holocaust Memorial
an dieses atemlose blinde Spiel...Rilke

It is permitted to move through the field of steles,
on foot only at a decorous pace.
The younger children dart among the flat
grey cement boxes, the steles,
climb the lower ones and leap
from each to each, set at the perfect distance.
Among the taller ones deeper in the field
where the path rises and falls with the footing uncertain
and the light narrows to a thin line above.
Children play peek-a-boo and older kids
snap digital photos poking a head out
or a bare leg with giggles and cell phone
videos to preserve themselves forever
and now and then a child will disappear.

The guards shoo off an older girl who stands
on a stele, another lying down. Both forbidden.
A lost child reappears on the far side
at the corner of Hannah-Arendt-Strasse
and Ebertstrasse and returns shouting
"I'm here, over here," unpuzzling
his friends. *Do not make loud noises,*
or shout or yell. No portable radios. No
lying or standing on the steles. No
jumping from one to another. No sunning
in bathing suits. No skateboards.
Do not dirty, soil or pollute. Commands
of the Security Officer must be obeyed.
And parents with their children refuse to vanish.

September 3, 2009

A Wedding

Hallowed by the marriage clerk at City Hall
they stand at the top of the broad marble stairs
for snapshots by their friends.
No parents around. They come from elsewhere
and by alien custom dress like church folk
for this civil fix. She holds his palm to her breasts
with one hand, the other rests low on her belly
which, under the sumptuous red dress
appears from her gesture to hold a child.
He looks at her, enfolding, mild.
They could be Rebecca and Isaac
founding a tribe in a strange land
or Hector and Andromache, thick
with their people, blind to the brute hand.

Wooden Crucifix 15th Century
il miglior fabbro

Both legs are gone below the knees
and the left arm, half the right remains
reaching outward, cross gone; not yet
slack in death the mouth is open in pain
and the sunken eyes downcast—
an ordinary church ornament
by John the German that lost its church

and now against a white wall, its horror
unmasked, stripped of the promise of comfort
for the common heretic of our murderous era,
it is just a human body locked in pain
beyond pain, remade as art
by Time, the greater artist, using
amputation and erosion.

The Natural, Brooklyn, 1950
for Hal Wohl

He was so far beyond anything we dreamed
in strength, speed or skill

by our bodies for ourselves, I knew
he was designed for marvels.

He seemed beautiful. It would be years before
we connected that to girls.

We were unaware of them and still very pure.
No point playing ball

with him, since he won everything effortlessly
in the natural course, like nightfall

waiting sweetly, lightly, in the end-zone
after scoring a goal.

He was shy and seldom spoke, and I was wordy
but could not imagine him dull.

I don't recall his face but I remember his thigh,
the shock of seeing it swell

with a man's strength under strain, no longer a boy's,
alien, beautiful, fearful.

Haystack

Out of the high window of a barn, leaping
into the scintillating hay-dust air
and landing again and again on a tall
pungent stack of hay—I forget where—

in the sweat-gleaming summer heat
full of the sweet smell and the rush of space,
flight and fall, the prickles on my skin,
with a playmate whose name and face

I can't recall—just shared ecstasy.
I don't recall the *me* there. Who was this boy?
Everything has vanished from that lost place—
but empty, pure, impersonal joy.

My Gallery

*This I drew using a mirror; my likeness
when I was still a child.* No self portrait
since so honest. My great skill so young
can still amaze me. Then I became profound
and beautiful, alas—curls, soulful stares.

Then before the mirror, I sat with a burin
or etching needle in my hand, the mirror
a tool of vision, and made faces, shouted,
scowled, in velvet hats, sailor hats,
with swords, plumes, my tools, my self
the available cheap model—whatever I was,
there I was, learning my craft, studying
myself inventing myself. Delight in this.

Then in the ornate curves of a tray that holds
the head of John the Baptist, I painted myself
in barely noticeable tear drops, my face
reflected upside down beneath the head,
blood gone from the face and rinsed from the beard.

Then in a fur hat and gold chain
before the easel, palette in hand, what broad
workman's hands I had at the height of my powers.
Great command in my forthright stare,
letting you feel my power and shake in my presence.
Thick hair. Strong chin. Nothing
required me to lie about myself except myself.

Then with a wild friend plunging ahead
while I with a fixed smile see the world
before us—only look! Only at her
naked to the waist, whose brown eyes
follow us around the room, her fingers

parted in the drapery gathered over her crotch,
demure but candid, incomprehensible
my world without her.

And always the pressure against the art of my time
that wants me to abstract myself and fold
into a pattern in which I stay hidden.

Then with a rag wrapped around my head to keep
the mess of paint out of my hair, I am
the rumpled one trying to see through spectacles
resting securely halfway down my nose.
The trying, the effort, the tentative, the seeing.
The things on the table that lie still to be seen.

Then I switched the taste for "picturesque
dilapidation" from old houses by the sea
or ancient farms to my own quilted face.
I wore outlandish costumes that as I aged
had nothing to do with me: a Pasha clown
with strong hands, and a face on which my life
was written, uneasy and curious,
from which I looked out calmly. I love my work,
I have not wasted my life. I can leave it.

The Forerunners

They tumbled like bright plastic bags blown
across the green campus
of the circus school, as I stopped in a line of cars
to watch the young clowns
soar across the road full sail in gowns and robes,
a day-glo rainbow of fright wigs,
rag doll goggle eyes, miming hilarious noises
in eye-filling silence
while they kicked a ball and tossed a hay-stuffed torso
back and forth as they ran
a heedless, headlong high-leaping swarm
around my car, and I saw
their ball was my own head, smiling, balding,
streaming brilliant ribbons
fluttering blood red, my body the stuffed thing
spilling balls of foam
that they tossed around, dressed in my usual rags,
jeans and baggy shirt,
flying like a cartoon ghost from hand to hand
and my death a hilarious game.

Remains

Near his death Chuang Tzu's disciples asked
why he chose tree burial in the ancient style
instead of a dignified grave. "Why," he said,
"do you favor worms to birds?" And so
they built a platform in a giant bo tree,
prepared a tissue thin muslin shroud,
and when he died they fed him to the birds.

In the Hope for Resurrection Cemetery
the master stone carvers and the rich
commemorate their beloved dead
by black stone angels with drooping wings
and shrouded faces or by crowds
of fat cherubs rising heavenward
as willows weep on slate for the city poor.

The long married mingled ashes on their lawn.
She warned us, "Watch for the wind.
I don't want you to brush me off your shoes."
Now, bone ash and bits of bone, they join,
laid in a yin-yang sign on terminal moraine
sinking in turf, touching and not, in one
pattern enduring through the next ice age.

Our ashes will be scattered in our lake,
where settled in the muck they may ascend
the ladder of natural hunger, plankton
to minnows to rainbow trout that lure
our voracious melodious loons
who in late fall will carry us through the skies
at ninety miles an hour to open water.

IV

Subway

The station platform, clean and broad, his stage
for push-ups, sit-ups, hamstring stretch,
as he laid aside his back pack, from which
his necessaries bulged, as he bulged
through jeans torn at butt, knee and thigh,
in deep palaver with himself—sigh,
chatter, groan. Deranged but common.
We sat at a careful distance to spy
on his performance, beside a woman
in her thirties, dressed as in her teens—
this is L.A.—singing to herself.
How composed, complete and sane
she seemed. A book by the Dalai Llama
in her hands, her face where pain and wrong
were etched, here becalmed, with faint chirps
leaking from the headphones of her i-pod.
Not talking. Singing, lost in song.

Driving Westward To San Diego

Plutonic rubble, boulders, gravel,
dust storms, sandstorms, stone and bone dry
desolation, post-nuclear waste, post-fire-storm,
the tors and pillars of a city we erased
with fire from the air. Human work.
But we are blameless for this dead debris.
The earth's heart, under its thin skin,
with magma red intensity,
overheats its igneous rock
beyond the limits of our own ferocity.
Driving westward on the interstate
above the east escarpment of the Coastal Range
we cross the ridge into a lush valley
green with Pacific rains,
land that seems like God's work,
in whose name we killed for it and cleared it:
lining streets with oleander, almond,
rows of ginkgo, fig, euphorbia,
white moons of giant clematis,
domesticated flames of rose and lily beds,
undulating fence lines, squared-off farms,
nothing here but what we ourselves devised,
all dimensions ample and humane.

Point Lobos

I saw it with my own eyes
before I saw the photographs.
We were there in the fifties
before the paths were roped
and a mule deer fawn
crouched in the brush as we neared
and hardly breathed though it shone
like the bright orange lichen
on the cypresses the winds
bent, lined and twisted.
I climbed above the coves
a hundred feet above
the violent surf immersed
in the calligraphy engraved
on tree and sand and stone
by storm blast and sea.

It was later that Weston taught me
to see how natural light reveals the world,
the minute graduations of the world's skin,
sand dunes, decaying peppers, bodies
of women folding on themselves
or opening as they do not
when they are arranged as art—
a world, sexual and formal in its folds
and the sensuous geometry of its body,
water, sand, stone, as living forms
and light discovering the force
that disorders and orders them all.

What design! Photographs, writing with light,
the maker's hand changing nothing;
no Vermeer applying light to a wall
to silhouette the shaded side of a girl's face,

pouring it on loaves of bread, a girl's arms,
a pitcher from whose dark she pours light.
Light in the pearl chambers of the nautilus,
not scattering but held within it,
on the sea in a dark cove, flashes of foam
arranged as if we could see the lines between them,
a woman's body, shaded and lit,
resting on sand with its light rising to greet her.

A Treatise On Ungovernment
Que sçais-je? Montaigne

A white haired man in a rich cloth coat
paces gravely on the platform waiting
for the Number 1 train, his hands
splay open with quiet eloquence
and he speaks to one absent to us
with the sound of a breeze through leaves.

What can not be understood can not be governed. Plato

A young couple, faces nearly touching,
speak to one another in Bengali
and Bengali flavored English, giving the words
a new music, with faces lifted
from Indian paintings
into American clothes, on a New York
street corner, waiting for the light to change.

What good are roots if you can't take them with you. Gertrude Stein
...a nation is the same people living in the same place. L. Boom

As the train lurches through its dark curves
a young woman grasping the pole
swings towards me in my seat
and her large breasts sway in a lacy
open-knit white blouse and nearly brush my face
offering an intangible perfume.

"Rabbi, Rabbi," she cried.
"Do not touch me." John, xx,16-17

He knows the city in intimate bits:
store windows, empty streets, a man
seated on a doorstep in front of a store,

a woman in a window overlooking rooftops,
a couple settling in their red plush seats
in formal clothes, before the theater crowd
presses in. An usherette against the wall.

*Canonically conjugate variables are pairs of properties, like position
and momentum, energy and time, linked in such a way that they
cannot both be measured at the same time.* W. Heisenberg

Accident. The torn boy dies, shattered, under
pressure bandages, pouring IV's, morphine,
the paramedic knows if he were someone else,
a surgeon, somewhere else, the OR,
the boy mangled in the road would live.

Omniscience is a fantasy of total power. Max Faust
The city is ungovernable. J.V. Lindsay

Shaving the outer skin of his fingertips
with a plastic lady's razor a thin man
with a gray stubble beard and hair—
is he a safe cracker preparing to feel within
the lock a delicate shift, or a lover
getting to the most sensitive layer
for the most intimate caress? What
would he not discover with those fingers—
what rods, tumblers, oiled wards.

Knowledge is Power. Bacon
With much knowledge there is much suffering. Rublev

"To confirm the conspiracy they wanted,"
he said over his moonshine martini,
"the intelligence was crap and we
couldn't move on it but we needed
to plant stories around the world so we confirmed

64

what we knew was crap, and all the newsmen
swallowed corrupt intelligence and the war."

On s'engage puis on voit. Napoleon

Because he revered their music, its plunge through his heart
and legs and throat in endless reverberation,
and their temples that flaunt in stone women entwined
with men, homage to flesh, and their philosophical mind,
cathedrals in which the stone flies upward like fire,
he was sure the population would not endure
the government roundups, pre-dawn arrests,
barely clandestine slaughter of whispering opponents
and the ruling thugs being merely a brief transition
out of confusion to a new suitable order
reflecting the soul of the people, his own soul,
so he endured for years in disciplined silence
and inner exile and when he refused to raise
his voice in total assent his total silence.

All wars are boyish and are fought by boys Melville

Stumpy silhouettes against bright windows
of a megastore way down the street—no light
between three figures, young boys in a clump
arms flailing and punching and one breaks
away and charges back full force
into the cluster of boy with windmilling arms
and another tumbles back then plunges in.
I'm too far away to see if it's a game
or fight or a game of fighting, proving themselves
against the bodies of others, two boys
against one or all against all.

The future is what happens behind our backs. The past is what we face. v. Marinetti

Memorial

> They are the dead you cry to. *The Trojan Women*

Outside, carpenters dismantle a scaffold,
a coppersmith seals gutters and flashing, a mason
tuck-points the uprights, smoothing.
Inside, all leaps skyward,
tall gothic arches rising
from thin pillars, spandrels of air,
a wall of air to carry the delicate vaulted roof.

The bronze spear through armor, sword
slashing through the neck, roadside
explosives of increasing ingenuity, in the market
intelligent human bombs, collapsing
lungs in cities in flame, or heat
and blast so great that bones burn
and nothing is left of the body to mourn.

As we walk around bantering
with craftsmen we wonder how
a town with only farms and a small mill
and summer people crowded around a lake
 produced such solemn beauty,
a cage where wind sings, a vault of air
to bury what vanishes.

Managed Grief

She accepts her grief, now that he is dead,
in miniscule doses. Her health demands
a touch of suffering. The soul expands—
Sophocles said so. Saint Paul agrees.

And what is healthy in her balance,
in that tall sturdy-to-elegant bearing
and coiled yellow hair,
makes me hate health. Boundaryless grief

is the debt we owe to love, and the death of her man,
my friend, at the height of his strength
will not, when tucked in the pocket
of an old coat in the attic, keep her heart intact.

Obit

I read the obit page. I am a devotee of the form—
the curved shape of the lives it creates, ample urns
turned by the hand muddling in the clay pit.
His country boyhood, battles with the occupying powers,
then with his countrymen, disciplined political anger,
his scattered ungovernable lovers, late statesmanship
that moved Ireland somewhere, death with mourners
filling the squares of Dublin. The chess rhinoceros,
whose roaring impatience with false moves and late moves
vanished after near death surgery, change of heart,
beloved figure and father before he died, mourned.
Consoling stories. Or not. Bitter or enervated endings
also part of the form. The ping-pong champion
    loved by Mao,
disgraced by the children of the Cultural Revolution
    for believing
in winning, swept streets in Beijing, rescued
by the Gang of Four, then thrown again in jail and forgotten
by all. A pilot who took one wild risk, flying his plane
over the length of the deck of the carrier he just torpedoed
whose guns all faced outward who returned with
    his wounded crew
and a plane with five hundred bullet holes. It is
    the obviousness
of his dash that struck him, no one had dared before
its crazy logic that worked and fame confused him.
All the stories have the same ending imposed by the form
that comforts and prepares one for completing the shape.

Old Home Day

Some rode in from farms at the edge of town
or flew in from work in the South and West
to gather around the Common, and the kids
lay down their frisbees for the cloud parade
of life as it's always been with nothing to change—
volunteer firemen and ambulance brigade,
the town cop, vets of foreign wars,
some recent ones that snared the world
with bombs, drones, mortars, BARs.
The wars against their own lead the parade,
vets of the Revolution and Civil War, Texas
against Cheyenne, King Philip's War,
with their flintlocks, muskets, sabers, arrows, bows,
and the band played and the beer flowed like blood,
in this sweet town where everyone knows
everyone's public name and secret name
and all their dead and no one locks their doors
or stands back to see. All join
this unbounded democracy.
Two brothers dead in one campaign
mosey over, AWOL as usual, for beer
and to read their names on the bronze plaque again
fixed to an obelisk in the square.

Sweet Town

When she reached her hand out the car window
to greet me I surprised myself with the hunger
with which I kissed it. I surprised her too.
Her car stopped at an angle at the corner
and her small yellow trailer stopped a fleet
of trucks which backed up all the cars on State Street.

Oh pardon, I beg the horn-wielding driver
(yelling "Ball her!") for causing all this strain
(I will kiss her hand only!) in sweet Montpelier
that uses the scramble system at State and Main
for getting us safely across for my (see above)
disorderly stun at untimely love.

The Gossips

They nod their heads in rising coffee steam
full of their grasp of the soul in its dark phase,
their gift for sudden intimacy
and startling sympathy when Linda lies
down with that dog George, they understand
how she couldn't but must and does
and then all the young gargoyles fall
through the razor steel net they make
for her and George, that rat, and fat, and swell-
headed and his wife says impotent to Jill
and what can either see in such empty
things. Honor the passion to know
in their talk, the art of making portraits
from negatives where dark makes light and light
dark. My beloved, even your
soft face floats in their talk, furrows
deepening between your eyes, wary,
not free of fault, loving secrecy,
secretly proud of your manifold disguise,
trusting their sympathy. They rarely lie
and will unmask you with effortless disloyalty.

Leaving The Body

His soul rose above his body as it ran
the full court forward toward the key.
No one throws it the ball or sees it in the clear
as it plunges forward yelling "I'm free, I'm free!"

He looks down at this galloping figure
unnoticed, breathless, enmeshed, deeply gone
in fakes and weaves, clamoring, pounding the boards
as he drifts away from his body carrying on,

and he wonders, looking far down,
whether he could love or even care
for that fiery animal, its animal brain
calculating its fruitless moves, a boy
beginning to decompose everywhere
in his brief fling at energy and joy.

Repeats

    Stunned by the lamp above my desk, a moth
landed on my glasses. I snapped my head
so sharply I hurt my neck and stopped work
on a small poem that didn't matter. The moth,
black with a smudge of iridescent green
underneath its thorax and orange head,
danced in the air and settled on my page.
I watched my neighbor's grandson toddle around
with an orange pail upended on his head
and bump into the parked car and laugh,
into the door and laugh and fall and laugh,
learning the hard and opaque by seeing nothing
and loving the feel of it, understanding nothing
of how serious comedy is, how odd to laugh.

Fugitive's Night Song

No blood spilt,
no patrols.
On the dark blue tiles
a mattress and quilt,
in the whispering, crowded room
when you arrive,
your family all alive,
you home.

David And Saul

Observed discreetly by members of the court
when David sings Saul grasps his spear.
The pundits blame Saul's madness,
but others, outside the court, say it's power—
the god-talk and the liberating tunes
enrage Saul as David sings.
His flagrant dazzle, rapture and spells
trivialize the authority of kings.
Saul gnashes his teeth, knots his face.
Think of poor Stalin, unable to kill
lucky Shostakovich. If not for the music,
if it were just poems, he could kill.

V

Pieces For The Suicide Of Paul Celan

When Celan asked Heidegger, who was Rector of the University of Freiberg in the early Hitler years, about his post-war silence concerning his Nazi past, Heidegger either refused to answer or was evasive. George Steiner says, "Either way, the effect on Celan must have been calamitous."

Roundness of eyes between bars
greets
the snake in the spine
the wolf in the heart

That mind is so naked
and the room is dark

you are allowed to touch it

that appearance of nakedness
under an impenetrable code

He cannot speak to you
not even tell you this
it would tell too much
and all of it wrong

distorted phrasing
the hesitations badly
out of place

Illegible, this
world, it all doubles

He asked the Rector:
Why did you assist
the cursed marriage

of the mutable state
to the immutable spirit—it drives
the one mad as the other dies

The Rector was
so committed to unity
of the whole, the body
was the state, the lovely
discordant University
allowed one voice only,
under the single will of the state
the whole as meaningless
to itself as a tree

to overcome the insult
of diversity

> (Look at them sullen
> on their bunks, some
> facing left, some right,
> or staring at your eyes, your throat)

and answered the aphorist
of image with silence

locked in his own depths
and climbing out
forever

August:

Is that a bird?
No, it is the brightest of the leaves
falling early

The last interrogation was unclear
the translator belonged to the court
no one understood
what the prisoner said—
he was carrion in a dog's mouth,
eaten, puked up and eaten again

Why are you waiting? Sew,
sew it on, he's torn
away his face, if you wait
too long the face will rot
the sutures won't hold
you know why he tore it
and why he wants it back

At The Frick

His eyes are narrowed not to miss a cue
for what to say that Henry wants to hear—
the ingratiating, serviceable face,
the richly furred language of the body
open and welcoming—Thomas Cromwell
by Holbein. Then Holbein's Thomas More
with a steady, penetrating glance, mouth
set in a skeptical turn, all wariness,
having a self to possess, possessing it.
Both men painted from life, alive
in the same room again, in New York:
More resisting the King, Cromwell saying
(no euphemisms, no disguises)
just what the King wants: Kill More.

The Execution Of Lady Jane Grey
(after a painting by Paul Delaroche, 1795-1856)

    Under a blindfold the girl is drugged by panic
    as her hands grope for where she must lay her neck.
    One Waiting Woman hides her face against the wall.
    Another faints. The headsman looks on, professional,
    concerned to make a clean job for a queen,
    and the priest reassures her about her sudden return
    to God as he guides her hand to the block. Everyone
    is beautifully dressed. The stage lights are on Jane.

    How deeply pathos suffuses the scene. No
    blood yet, no wall of flaming jet fuel racing across a room
    driving you out the ninetieth floor window.
    No roll call to witness a hanging, on your forearm
    no numbers. I thought at first: how did they find four
    empty planes? I could not imagine passengers.

Ignorance

Straight black hair, olive skin,
South Asian or North African, her mouth
too composed for sensuality, with no sign
of which passion's under that composure
she struggled for. She was so beautiful
chatter hushed when she entered.
After a swig of murky tea from a bottle
in her pack, she settled herself in her seat
on the Piccadilly line, closed her eyes
and sank in meditation on the clattering train,
her hand working away in a bag, small and gray,
she had tied to her wrist with a ribbon
and beaded string, perhaps telling beads,
perhaps setting the time for the bomb in the pack
on her lap—perhaps readying her soul
for reward in paradise. But I did not flee
the train, or that subway car, or even move
farther off. My ignorance of her mind
behind that quiet beautiful face was perfect.
I trusted that stillness and stayed still.

—London, 2006

Carmens, The Audition
>*Jamais Carmen ne cédera!*
>*Libre elle est née et libre elle mourra!*

Enter two ill matched women
casting for Carmen—the law of their beauty
occludes the safety codes
designed to protect and torment.
One is soft-featured, soft-bodied,
blonde, unpracticed, yielding,
a fine singer spoiled by her gift,
the Carmen you forgive everything,
a victim of her power she fails
to understand: innocent
arrogance, instinctive freedom,
the wound that invites the knife.
We weep for her. The other
a studio tan brunette, focused
lean face, tight mouth,
eyes that master the whole room,
knows her desires and gets them met.
Freedom requires power and she grasps it
but doesn't. Carmen will never yield.
She was born free, she will die
free, boasts Carmen of herselves,
who dream that they choose,
but do not expect to die
ever, nor understand their enemy:
its secure possession thwarted,
love murders.

From *The Book Of Blessings*

Hear, O Israel, the divine abounds
everywhere and dwells
in everything: the many are one.
The blind giant swells

proceed across the dispassionate ocean
and scour shores of tree
and house, of humans and their works—
without conscience or memory—

with divine indifference. Rampant cells
in lung and brain and breast
are fruitful and multiply the same divine
unconcern for their withering host.

The divine abounds in the press of bodies
where touch increases terror—
driven with clubs into a dark room—
divine—the tight door

that seals behind them—their prayer
whose echo tumbles and roars
in the cement room—divine the gas—
divine the man who pours.

The Entitled
The Duke of Brevière and his brother the Duke of Cumberland
painted by van Dyck

Two boys, fair curled hair, brash eyes,
jewels and gold embroidered clothes (the lace
alone would feed all the poor of London)
are a vision of self-pleasure and assurance.
Their necks are long and slender, their arms thin,
their fingers crusted with rings and long.
It is not their strength we see but comfort
with their weakness. They will ruin
everything they touch and fail without pain.

Toad Skin

On a dirt road, a paper-thin dry thing
like a black parchment cut-out of a toad
in mid-leap, partly sideways, drawn by a master,
now boneless, as if it never had bones.
Only the tough skin survived the flattening
by one of the rare cars here. Poor unwary thing.
How much of us will last, tough, stiff,
cured by summer sun. Our better towels
outlast our flesh. Are Nazi lampshades
holding up? Shrunken heads? Mummies?
A few poems. Stone monuments. Some bones.

Mountain Lion
for John Peck

He flattens his haunches deep
into the brown leaves--
invisible under the ferns
on the cool forest floor.
It is inescapably clear
he's here—his yellow eye
marks every step I take.

I carried my thirty-eight
for six months after I caught
sight of him crossing the road
until I felt foolish and quit.

Like the stealthy Bengal tiger,
driven by hunger, not rage,
he's a merciful cat when he kills
with one spring from behind
and one bite to the neck.

Bengali woodcutters wear
a backward facing mask
which baffles the tiger's spring
while the woodcutter walks to safety
praying and trembling—the tiger,
impotent, stalking behind him.

I'm resigned to the reign of the cat.
He allows my trek through these woods
with provisional forbearance
but I shake in his real presence,

wait for him to learn
my desperate masquerade
and walk with a double face,
the one in front that ignores him,
that pokes my way through the trees,
and the one facing back that sees.

Learning From Nature

Stupid about exhaustion, no inner brake,
I was cutting up fallen live oak
in the Santa Cruz Mountains with a chainsaw
that as I tired, kept bucking past my ear
as I dodged its kickback, two or three times
through each hunk of firewood, and I looked up
and saw, circling so low above me
I smelt their breath, turkey vultures watching
expecting me to slice my thick skull
in two decisive final pieces. They saw
something I did not, with my old dogged style,
ignoring weakness, working till I fall,
and their carrion stink killed off my belief
that life was work and work life.

Meditations On Violence

Too near the ancient troughs of blood
Innocence is no earthly weapon.
                              Geoffrey Hill

Thou hast beat me out
Twelve several times, and I have nightly since
Dreamt of encounters twixt thyself and me—
We have been down together in my sleep
Unbuckling helms, twisting each others throat—
And wak't half dead with nothing.
                    Aufidius in* Coriolanus*

1

The History Of Doves In Our Time

The doves batter themselves against the big wind
but make no headway toward their nests in the eaves
and they circle and plunge and are driven back
above the roof like children trying to force
their bodies through a close police line
who are hurled back at every lunge and feint
and scramble up screaming and try again before
they scatter in terror as their parents cry out their names
from the other side of the line. The big storm
is racing across the wide plains where no trees
or hills slow its force, its wall of wind. It will be
an even worse time to be helpless and far from home.

2

"Being young," he said, dreading himself,
"persuaded it was right, too young
to tell, myself, if it was right,

I could do it knowing I had to do it—
I've known in football deadly competitive rage,
knowing the other team was vermin,
their lives or ours, and this knowledge
enabled me, enabled me to do and do...

"I've seen my uncles cry
over what they had to do in Vietnam—
burning men in holes, exploding bodies,
when they were both too young
as friends burned and burst around them.
And if I had to do it I could do it."

Then a capricious turn against his dread—
bravado, a strained smile, a cocked head.

3

THE HEALING ART
comical-tragical-epical-historical

When Prince Andrei dies, millions mourn,
each in his chair, alone, the great weight
of *War and Peace* resting in their hands,
reading of his wounds and fever
and the cruel tease—full life, young son,
great heart reopened after grief,
wrenched from him, and how severe
and inevitable his death appears—
though with his skeptical turn,
skill at handling intricate affairs,
he could have held back from battle.

Chekhov was enraged at Andrei's death.
He knew the modern way to drain infection,

that this death was medically unnecessary,
he, himself, could have saved his man.
Only a cruel art would contrive
(Oh, Tolstoi!) to kill Andrei.
He could have blinded him and let him live.

4

This handsome boy will die
because he must avenge
himself his father's murder
in a village near Durango.
Now he is here to study
in Palo Alto High
loved in the Quaker home
that shelters him from his past
by the frightened daughter who sees
in his silence his assent
to the unbetrayable task
and tastes the hate in his kiss.
His gifts will lead him on
swiftly through medical school—
not haunted but possessed
by the clear pastoral code
and the cool, simple skill
that rushes the dead man's son
to kill his father's killer
and tumble ahead in the race.
As he shoots the man at his table
he will make the same choice
his father's killer did
and leave the son alive
who, when he's fully prepared,
will kill him in his clinic
in a village near Durango

as he lances a child's boil
that splashes over his coat
while he looks up with annoyance
and dies with the same surprise.

5

Letter From Witwatersrand
    From a friend after the massacre at Sharpeville:

"The exit wounds were all in front. They issued
an order that stood me and a rifle
on guard from midnight to dawn over our
suddenly less venerable school.
If this rifle is stolen my sentence
is seven mandatory years. With my
wife and two children in the house
there's no doubt in which direction I
am forced to shoot. Understand, today
I'm damned. The wounds were all enormous.
Breasts and whole faces blown away."

Signed: *"Pudendum Africanus."*

6

Small Wars
    "Thank God for Numbers." Jane Austen on war news.

Dozens of deaths, only,
or a few hundred or thousand
we now call low intensity conflict:

we can obtain the totals—snipers
against tanks, bystanders,
skeletal children in torched villages.

To count is to grasp, to enable
a shattered body to enter
the stiffened mind. A solvent of sorts.

What we call great
or total war, is when we lose
count—several millions,

several, several millions
screaming, half on fire, crushed in rubble,
disappear innumerable.

7

AT THE MEMORIAL

I looked for one name, a former student
from the early 'adviser' years of the war
who derailed himself to Vietnam
in an aimless time, looking for something more
than a pallid student life at a seminar table.
I heard he died from one who heard he died,
so in faint columns etched in the dark wall
I searched for a name attached to a clever boy
and with slow repeated blows inside my skull
all those names attached themselves to people
as the numerousness gathered its human weight
joking and leaning on the table.

8

MACHINE GUN NEST
>In 1962, when this encounter took place, Paul Smith
>had recently retired from the *San Francisco Chronicle*.
>Under his editorship it had won many Pulitzer Prizes.

Every man was dead over his gun in this nest.
Eisenhower hauled the press corps there
to purge their cruel wit and urge them to awe
at this supreme devotion, said Paul Smith,
who was hauled there and awed.
He wanted to awe his high-minded guests
and their pretty students at his house on Partington Ridge
above Big Sur overlooking the violent Pacific.
(I was enchanted by its wilderness and elegance,
the rattlesnake disposed of on the patio with a shotgun,
the circle of tall, beautiful women in long
black handwoven dresses and gold cigarettes,
chic, bored.)
                    But we were Pacifists,
anti-tests-anti-war-anti-bomb
against "advisers" in Vietnam. Antic and active.
I could not get past my outrage
that no one could see clearly the this and that
to prevent the World War. Those men
should not have been there, draped on their guns
clogging them with blood. This was simple.
That simple. I denied their heroism.
Smith pounded on the table to make me see.
The students wandered away. Adults in battle
like parents' fights, were frightening,
and their lives also hung in this balance,
so I too shouted and would not see.

9

les enfants aussi, the children too: a notation in pencil
by Pierre Laval on the order for deportation of Jews from
Vichy France to Auschwitz

Plodding, with heavy luggage, in dark suits
before their patient wives, who, unruffled,
with broad Brooklyn accents, keep order
among their many children with orderly curls;
the older ones, decorous, mannerly,
thoughtful, subdued, *les enfants aussi*.

The fathers fold away their dark coats,
and bury themselves in men's work, study
and prayer. Our flight to London is crammed
with Orthodox American Jews and airline security
clamps down with rigor, figuring them
a doubly delicious target—*les enfants aussi*.

I am grateful for the long delay and the rumble
below in the baggage hold, and the explosive
sniffing dogs, better friends to man
than man. There are no innocents Americans, say
the scourge of infidels, who're free
with God's vengeance: *les enfants aussi*.

10

THE MASSACRE

The journalists lied about the numbers.
They said hundreds were killed,
unarmed, facing the world
with the force of their souls, and the wall

of guns, against all rules, opened fire.
Historians say that only 44 were killed.
Ramon was among them and he alone was 97 dead,
Roberto at a low estimate was 86,
and Arturo the precious whom everyone loved,
six of whose odes will last forever,
there is no counting the number of deaths of Arturo.

11

Photo Exhibit in Soho, Nov. 2001

There are few corpses here. What we are shown
is mourners and rescuers and the crime against real estate,
the firemen's priest killed performing the rites
over a fireman killed by a leaper, and then the leapers.
Mostly it's the massed communal grief
that multiplies the solitude of grief, faces
sobbing or seeking or stopped in unbelief.
Bloody survivors. The dead are what we breathe.

From Saint Venus Eve (1972)

The Listener Aspires To The Condition Of Music
for Janos Starker's performance of the Bach cello suites

Because a bow across a cello
moves with such precision that the strings
fill the air with that progression of exact
vibrations that ensnare the air, that hammer,
anvil, stirrup all transmit the movement
of, and move themselves, and move
the mind in such complex voluptuous
sensations, moving everything within to make
it dance its court and country dances in a
suite of dances no human body
ever danced or could dance, because
air will not support our heavy bodies,
something in us dances, lets us die
a little, making music of us, of the still
gross grounded lump that listens.

Flaubert And Emma Bovary

1

Everything I can't control, that slips,
rolls across the room and doubles back
with great weight and speed and heat—light
on great feet—a big cat—a bear—slack
when I expect resistance—tense when I don't—
in grasping you I hold, hold on to, back.

2

Only two sacraments have touched you:
communion and extreme unction. The rest
connect one with the world, but these, O these
are intimate, direct: the deafening breast,
clasped hands, the cross, kissing mouth
half open, bruising lips, the last, the best.

3

You are my banality and arsenic,
I gave you both: the stale
come of sentimentalists, the douche—
corrosive, killing. You are lying, pale
and sleepless everywhere in France tonight
and in my bed when I am most alone.

4

Have I devised you as my lover?
as myself? as both? Do those slim hands
prodding at your meat upon the plate
(bored, you brood on steaming beef, your man's
face) serve both of us in this dismembering sea
where everything dissolves into ourselves.

Noli me tangere

>Sustaining unbreathing poise, arms crossed,
>legs crossed and re-crossed, balancing
>our rigid bodies (O your shrouded breasts)
>our eyes evade and check with grim skill.
>
>Not touching. Stiff deliberate revisions
>of position: as precise as diplomats
>around, around their heavy chairs, or birds
>in flight that touch only to court or kill.

Nomos, Logos

...if there were nothing else in heaven to delight the eye but the great beauty of glorified bodies, that alone would be very great bliss... Saint Teresa of Avila

Prayer would be relief. No man,
husband or lover, will follow her
down, down to where she goes,
where flesh hangs like strung stones
on the arm and the numb hand knows
nothing to keep its cunning hold,
dropping book and glass and phone.

What she knows of ecstasy, the going
out, away, of breath, leaving
the vague point behind the eyes
clear and high and ringing, comes
by the window, seeing the field of snow
lucid in the dark, feeling the silence
scream in the leap of her cat
at the poised bird; or naked and cold,
shivering beneath a thin quilt,
staring at the fire.

Among her men, dissatisfied, perverse,
knowing they never know her where she lives,
she has a restless sense of where the arm
would fall around her, where the face
would touch her face, his few words.

Prayer seems the only way to call
the figure of a lover knowing all
down from his distances to her.
His touch will shake her, throw
power through her, make her rough body

move with grace among her pots and show
to her, in light, her own transfigured face.

Is there a name, a high clear trill
filling the mouth to bring him in,
tasting of him, resonant and full? Now,
the old search, the slow scrape down
to where he lives, where no name
will reach and no word serves
to invoke the wordless dark.

On Meeting The Blessed Virgin Jane Austen

To be seen for once with clarity!
by eyes so quick, only
the catch lights flicker, marking
my complacency and vanity
before I say "Of course, of course."

She'll note the way my eyes rip her dress
in search of friendly meat, but pass
and talk of Austerlitz, how numbers
(a mercy!) protect us
from contact with the merciless facts.

When I grouse about renting out
my house: "I am not fond
of the idea that my shrubberies
will always be approachable." she will,
how I pray for this, laugh down grace.

Padre Antonio Vivaldi

    Every day, even on the dog days,
    the fat Padre plays the harpsichord
    in the adobe courtyard. Children dance
    around him, race around that elegant
    inlaid instrument, around the lush trees
    whose broad leaves are nearly black. The yard,
    the high walls, are lurid—yellow as lemons.
    When Padre jumps up, runs, they never know
    whether he will join them in their ring,
    that stress of brilliant energy sustained,
    or pirouette florid and screaming.

Secret Love Song

Deliberate as statesmen we ignore
each other publicly. Within,
hilariously, we admire the skill
with which we play unconscious, cold.
Such hot, gay virtuosity!
With tomahawks and great hearts
beneath the bison robes and dark
poker faces at the powwow.

So cloaked, the need to speak out straight
or kiss the soft corner of your neck,
there, below the ear, will die.
Our elaborate dishonesty
lies like truth.

Speech On The Telephone

Here we are locked. Let all who think
that loving the indefinite
is easy, look at the cold, black
devices in our hands, listen
to us squeeze words out.

The Crow Down Comforter

>*Jusqu'à l'heure de l'oiseau noir*
>*Annonçant la fermenture légale du coeur."* Yvan Goll

Because you wife has run off with one man
only, count yourself among the fortunate.
>*Down a down, hey down a down*

You have discovered, simply, the limits
of trust and knowledge. Besides, he is like you.
>*hey down a down*

Consider him whose wife with clear eyes sailed
his Triumph into a motorcycle club.
>*Down a down*

...her wiry and disciplined body with shrill
cries to each delighted member.
>*hey down a down*

She acted out the joyful fantasies
of starvation and despair. Those at least are
>*Down a down*

He has discovered a further limit: that when
each of them loved noone, the other became noone. For love.
>*With a down derry derry derry down down.*

Paolo And Francesca

After she told their story with courtly dignity
and would retreat wordlessly I reached
out to seize her free arm and said:
"I must know more. Did you both tie
all those deaths together as you died
both on Giancotto's sword?
Did he burst out first, fumbling,
impatient at the ten years delay,
leaving you mothering or cold,
wondering after all, Why? Or were you
so overfull that you exploded,
screamed and flooded, sounding ring on ring,
to bring him in with you, amazed;
or to paralyze him, spin him back,
afraid of all that force? Or was it
a long farce of joint performances,
grinding in and in,
grating fatigue at the cold drill?
Or did you come with textbook tenderness,
at once together, one spirit making
one body there on the soft grass
dying with the sword?
The meaning of your deaths and the entire
gesture depends on this? Is it a fable
of the old imprecision of the flesh,
its frailty, absurdity, weak service,
or of its rare success?"
She whispered, "No matter. No matter."
And both bodies smoked away
into that boneless spiral of lovers.

The Judges

The judges twirl their fat mustachios about,
lick their lips red and toss their thick boots
over the arms of their archiepiscopal chairs.

The judges smooth and pat the ink-line bands
of hair on their flat scalps, tighten their
ambiguously wavy mouths and cross their legs.

The judges shake their white manes about
their white faces, fill their lungs and bellow
rising out of their deep chairs.

The judges clasp and unclasp their slender fingers,
compress their squealing teeth, force
their attention, attention and drilling eyes.

The judges brace their legs and separate
the long approaching line to left or right
along the railway platform, tapping
with a white baton the quick or slow.

The judges warm behind their glasses, smile
benign disingenuous smiles, their soft brown
curls and beards surround entangling questions.

The judges adjust and maladjust their ties,
impatient with some hot elaboration
riffled into their prim figures and facts.

The judges point distractedly to one bench
or the other, caress their quilted faces,
turn to check their files and lose their places.

The judges lean back, discreetly suck their teeth,
tap their paunches, count the flies in the webby
high window, hearing it all repeat and repeat.

The judge nods yes out of the warm light
behind him with wide eyes framed by the golden
glare; rests his left hand in the book on his lap
and reaches out his right relaxed and open.

The Scribe
Dynasty V, 2650B.C. (Louvre)

The limbs rest easily as long
settled stacks of logs; the face
is ready, tense with held breath;
a stretched poise about the mouth
and wide nostrils; eyes and ears are open jaws;
inlaid eyes of alabaster, black
stone, silver and crystal shine.
All the intake valves are open
with disciplined attention. This
is pure giving. Speak to him,
he listens and his eyes are suns.

Underneath their prints and weaves the girls
are naked. Under blue flannel shifts,
rough wool suits and suede, even under fur,
they have their furry places, snowdrifts
and warm alcoves where the cat curls.
When they move it all moves. Living under
vinyl coats, Egyptian cotton blouses, smooth
black silk sheathes it, keeps it warm
and ready for the hand. Beneath
the surfaces are surfaces, swelling, calm
varied with their seasons. Clothes conceal
like words and skin: what they cover (even Gothic
drapes, classic folds, baggy comic
slacks, starched habits) they reveal.

From Uncarving The Block (1978)

Uncarving the Block

You are the lowland. All streams
flow to you. Why do you stall me
with slim eurasian androgynes curling
and uncurling, gold silk blowing, on my fenders,
windshield, hood? Why, when my soul would plunge
through traffic do their quick fingers reach
through and tap staccato on my steering
wheel and scare my children with their peeping
tree-frog laughter? They jerk
their heads like electric dolls with crossed circuits.
They batter up thunder with their toy fists.
I have contracted to come to you in peace
but you gather these archaic images against me.
I will take them down to you. I will carry them.
I will come on foot.

You are the lowland. All streams
flow to you. I see you from where I am—
I am—standing, urgent, circling around you
circling around me, trying to talk
to you who never talk. How else
find you out?
Like when she left me in the restaurant,
walked out fierce—I was being thick,
swallowed slow and rose to the window.
In the plate glass, the bright room reflected
with all people eating; myself
stopped and clumsy, my shadow
the only dark place to see through.
I saw her figure in the watery street
move into many figures
moving. You walked behind
and through me. You are not gone. I stand
here talking to you.

You are the lowland. With a typed list
of witnesses I set out for you.
Eight pages in a packet, waterproof.
I will follow the large streams down
this spring thaw as they join
one another in their narrow stone beds
gathering to white violence screaming
through the too small passage through boulders
before they enter at last the slow river
that pushes along the valley floor. At the inn
they will file out to greet me. The innkeepers wife
will bring hot towels and the cook will retreat
to the wall. At the end of my stay I will be so changed
they will shove me off my cot. I will no longer
need the list of witnesses.

You are the lowland. All streams
flow to you. The road down is thick with fathers
yammering in claques, crowding, coming between
us and the clean descent, gristle clogging
our wheels, their bearings moan like cellos.
They want us to be water in the sea of them, lower
ourselves together into the reservoir,
enter together the sun and air. Never
in years do they move, they soak into the roads.
Behind, their bad-tasting, ill-fitting lives
we push into, eating our way through
the live stew of them, follow our teeth down
and our waists soften and we join new clubs
and they are twice dead as we begin.

You are the lowland. All streams
flow to you. Your mind flows obscurely; the pike
and minnow poking at the lotus root,
the catfish and the skittish trout, each
speckled stone, seem in their depths to play

upon its surface in a trick of bent light
or seem like one tessellated thing
seen faintly beneath its black skin.
Among your warm, worn-in shoe of a wife,
the lover that flew off in a cloud of insults
or the girl who climbs all over you in bed
you cannot and will not choose.
Now you can ask of love or stoned fucking:
which sinks deepest in you? Sounding
with both, keeping both within.

You are the lowland. All streams
flow to you. She said: To me. Yielding
to all like ice melting, descending
the ladder of love to the unloved body moving
within me, quite, worthless, low, I am
an empty space for all men to live in.
I burned the rich dresses that my father
gave me when I married, even the gold
embroidered silk. I left my husband to curse
in the house and keep it. The maids make faces at him.
I am a town under siege. The men, the pricks
within me dream of having me in peace,
each one a bully. I am most true
when most open to most men. They must
renounce me as I renounce them.

          All streams
flow to you. But the wardens of beautiful women
and beautiful men have wired ahead:
We and our wards are circling and circling. Stop.
How can we reach who cannot touch. Yours.
She said: O, mother, father—from Anne a nose,
from Willard his firm chin, from Nona hair—
I dove in, rose too long later, stiff,
doubled in size, leaky, unwieldy as a roped hog.

With Love. Stop. They have their own
silent signals, like *there's one, there's one,*
meaning not the hunter hot after game,
nor the hunted in panic away, but another game
where the slain one scrambles up and keeps on running,
enacted with decorous poise before their keepers
in the migrating wildlife preserve. Stop.

You are the lowland. I dreamed of visiting
and wound up talking to your husband
who couldn't catch my name.
My book swung open, each page
painted over, thick with muddy temperas.
I never wanted such obscene safety.
Our friends have new friends for you
and you relax again and lean
your chair against the wall, hold up
a wine glass and across your face
the slight smile, that in the half-
light of an empty restaurant
on a waitress stops my throat.
I carry you with me still. You are stuck
here in my throat.

              All streams
flow to you. Her tears. Her tears.
And they fuss about her with patient voices.
We cannot have our mothers or fathers
either naked or in their Christmas pajamas.
"And the Bishop, dear, is not for you,"
and there is no comfort for her and brother
and sister pour her more coffee. *A maid refus'd.*
The Archbishop comforts the Bishop
who knows his peace lies in his celibate life,
his house that is spacious and light, the garden
with rhododendrons, early and late,

their faint odor as he climbs the stairs
and the organ tone of bees in the bright acacia.
Rewards chill the service. You are the lowland.
In the tide pools the water eddies over
the rooted things that wave their thousand arms.

You are the lowland. All streams
flow to you. Disinter this poet
from his stone tomb in the family plot.
Enter and dislodge those poems he could not
bring himself to speak—addressed
to you. Reclaim them. Batter the stiffness
of his male will, his well mannered style.
With your small fingers and your harsh hand
get between his fingers, bend the wrist
forward, break his rigid fist open,
loosen his tongue with your tongue.
He died too young—was born old.
Look at those stiff pathetic gestures—
elbows stuck to his ribs. His walk.

You are the lowland. I play
tough with you, pretending you are weak
and running from your urge to throw yourself
with desperate abandon into me
or any man playing manly.
You hold my arm in this play leaning
into me. Your gravity
is desperation under great restraint.
On my oak arm your hips swing like slack rope.
But this is my play. I play both parts. You
stay shy and smile like an amused infant,
return each marking stone, let the jungle return
and renew your burnt over garden as you burn
and clear another and let me grow back

a tree seedling. I will be, finally
a mother of gardens.

You are the lowland. All streams
flow to you. But Rich didn't know
he was in line or that there was a line
and he wasn't ready when his time was up
and there he was with his pants around his knees
and the light spinning and was whacked
real hard in the back of the head and roared
and the lady said "You next" and he reached out
to keep from falling down the stairs and he fell
but by the time he was halfway down it didn't matter
and he didn't know if he'd see his parents there
and his kids didn't know beans about the business
and they didn't even have a shroud
and no one knew how to make one.

You are the lowland. So I lay me down
filled up with strychnine to retire
to wanting one thing only, thus
consigned to planning in a rational state,
a quadruped family, a daily grind
and hired heart; stretched
out myself since no sudden breath-
taking convulsion stretched me,
involuntary torsion cracking bone and
tendon with its going-out-of-place
and woke refreshed.
My daughter and my boss smile over me.
My son and wife are busy in another room.
My friends, my students, mill and grind downstairs
and I have swallowed something and survived.

You are the lowland. All streams
flow to you. In respect to which the rash

Sennacherib spoke of Babylon this vaunt:
the city and its houses, from foundation to tower,
I destroyed, I devastated, I burned with fire.
The wall and the outer wall, temple and gods,
I razed and dumped them into the Arakthu Canal.
Through the midst of that city I dug channels,
I flooded its site and made its destruction complete
for the cool image of the fire on the wide canal,
to sail on, to seize a girl on, to feel like god's
katabolist, possess the girl, sink the hacked body
in the Canal, scattering the ghost
out of its hammering channels. No god
is complete unless his power is complete
and we cook our own pigs over our own fire.

You are the lowland. All streams
flow to you. Seated according to the Law,
or standing. Without wine. This is not Eros
we pray to who would prefer Sennacherib
with his crazy goyim and their horses.
We woo you with elbows on a desk
one leaves for more coffee only; driven
from gardens and gardens; turning
spirit into food in circuses; dying
together in sealed rooms; celebrants
with tears at the old wall. We civilize
ourselves to civilize you. Here is your book.
These are the letters of your name.
An owlet staring at an owl. Why
the silence and the carrion stinking breath?

You are the lowland. And I am a scrap
blowing about between friends
down the stairs with Marvin
across the parking lot with Harry Oster
up the hall to Don and back

to something I need to know from Stavros:
all the time watching names change,
sniffing fenceposts, tongue slavering
down, aimless dog, maybe,
but earnest, earnest; protected thereby
from a sedentary life.
This is the pleasure of the housefly
following its own serious nature, hidden
from us this joy. Nothing has no name.

           All streams
flow to you. Like the roofer moving
so still I didn't know he was a human
till he passed across a beam; like the three
retired workingmen in Moline with faces
like radar screens installed over guns watching
the young reporters zip babbling into the *Times
Democrat* as a wedge of clouds passes
reflected off a wet stone. Checked
unwrinkling shirts stretched down into their vast pants.
They don't move to get where they will go,
where they want to go, into the river of wind
that moves within the susurrating trees,
sunset coming on Stonehenge, breaking red
sidelong on grey, making the stones flesh.

You are the lowland. All streams
flow to you. You hesitate like one
wading in a quick stream, each stone
unsure with wet moss under foot
in the tangling and untangling water.
Tentative, tentative,
   your hand is on the door which opens to you,
you are a deer among the flowering
alfalfa, engorged with all that green and yellow,
with those vulnerable eyes alert,

swinging about, alert. All sinew and surprising
softness yielding. And to that courtesy, she yields
letting her robe, her arms long and thin, fall,
an Easter lily falling open. This we call
marching without moving.

                I dream of falling
with breath held to the never arrived at
moving impact point, desperate arms
against air in which I don't fly
dropping from the giant parent,
towering ice-box, skyscraper, down.
Below you, nothing. No fall is possible
from your low richness, your alluvium,
in which every live thing rots
to richness, greenness, brightlaced,
the music of the duck, cock, squirrel, the scream
of the weasel, bee-hum, the faint curled trail
of crawlers, many dark eyes, my children.
You are the lowland. Tall grass and lines
of silver poplar in the black earth. All streams
flow to you.

EPITHALAMIUM

Reaching out with long distance calls
to say hello, fly in for brandy, movies,
spiced wine by candlelight,
to watch the storm across the valley
close in, a face to lean across
the table to, whose skin is here
at your fingertips, or for your hand,
or new woods for you to enter
to scout out its clear places
where the deer graze,
reaching out to bring in.

Bringing in, with the piano, hauled
by farm boys, with rugs, pots, soiled
work clothes, red clay on grey,
the wedge of sky between the elm top
and the roof, alien proteins,
her hair in your teeth, the bridge
of her nose pressed into your neck,
the curve of her at rest, wholly
within you between sleeping and waking,
that you smile her morning smile
and she stares your stare,
bringing in to keep.

Keeping. You are ashamed to speak of it:
that you would own her the way she
owns you, and would destroy
the wingèd life to keep that picture of you
in her eyes intact through blinks and sleeps
to death. Speak of it the way
the clay plaque keeps the print of gears,
this grave rubbing keeps
the knight and lady in their formal stance

who are their own background and foreground;
the eye open, the mouth, the hands, open to receive
and give and keep giving.

ANTETHALAMIUM

Unsafe, I place myself in this design
here behind my two eyes, secured.
How else not obtrude.

You drag away from me, a disconsort
of musicians following, their antique instruments
new minted for your sparse rites.

They tune up now in random discords
for the serenade to raise your new fort.
All this is done indoors.

And you stare only at the floor, your eyelids
lovely as your eyes. Look, the oriental carpet
has an extra fish, half a circle.

The bridesmaids and friends are irrepressible,
all leers, bawdy songs and snickers.
No mystery in this dry ritual,

only a man with whom you do not fear
desire, for by desire is the world revealed,
you say, not knowing how the world is hidden.

Burying A Child (R.B. 1969-1974)

    With smeared mascara and a dripping nose
    her mother follows an aunt around the city
    searching, searching, and more remote
    than ever her father is just another echo
    in the abandoned house and the rabbi
    chided us as willfully blind
    who, when called, slid our spadefuls of dirt
    down the side of the grave and did not
    dump them on that still resonating box.

Famous Lovers

They seem like the pious from the old world,
no wavering, just a forward trudge,
black broad hats, black coats
sweeping around them, their eyes fixed ahead
past our stares, on course
among our perilous dividing minds
through the door of home and close the door.
Hidden from us their slow hands, their exultation
at the long disrobing search for someone there
moving the skin under the sliding cloth
raising the arm to glow against the light
naked within the habit of passion.

Last Act: Don Giovanni

He understood no other name but death
for the wish to be restrained. The Stone Guest
invited in defiance clomped across the room
and the massed silver quivered on the table
at each footfall, the last feast
to end the comic murderous lust and send
Giovanni and his phallus errant
cursing through the trap door and stage flames.

He had no inner life—no check and counter—
an animal attack against the law
without love, with one drive only,
to push into the soft door, either
open in passion or closed and dry in terror.
He was a numbers man: a finite
linear series that comprehends its end.

Let us pray for him.

For his eyes whose rolling hunger we have guessed,
let them (Amen) close and ears that heard
much squealing in the highest register
of acquiescence, though protest was music too,
hear, after your applause, nothing more (Amen).
It is said he missed much loamy richness
because he kept his nose stopped with wax
though this is an addition to the text
by the too fastidious and he was not.
Let it now be stopped (Amen). His mouth,
what it tasted of other mouths, and his lies—
how sweet they must have sounded—how much like
civilized duplicity—on their account
forebear and wish that mouth its dry peace (Amen).
The hands that alone or with others gave

much pleasure, and received, and agony,
let their bones brown richly among their rings
forever undisturbed (Amen) and feet
that pointed downward for release rest now
not splayed, relaxed, but propped (Amen) upright.
And for the instrument whose instrument he was,
let it decline into perpetual rest, the terror
he dreamed of. He was his own instrument.

Our Other Mind Problem

We have learned a mandarin language,
an ingrown puzzle binding us
to talk to one another—
the many ones and others—to disengage

with unfixing clarity our actual selves
as figures from their grounds, the sheets
of glass or broad leaves that hold rain
like beads of sweat on the high arched,

double arched, Romanesque brow
that vaults above your eyes, half closed
to disarm. Your face in my hands,
the ground for now of all figures of you

dancing in this small circle to shifting
rhythms, with abrupt counterturns
to a Renaissance court. And I,
always a something else thereby.

"Dere hart," you say, "how like you this?"
and you are Anne Boleyn, tragic,
for the moment gay, with young
Thomas Wyatt, ironic gentleness

moving a dazed self into your bare all.
A cavalier? No, a stumbling grenadier
impaling under her dress
his favorite camp girl after a brawl

or his wife, unsafe at home
in coarse cotton, waving fat arms
spilling the wine, cursing! cursing!
That mourning woman of Lorenzo

secure among her signs,
the veil, the empty ring, the lines
of funereal cypress inside the walls
of her dead lord's demesne.

Her mesocosm, manor, pasture, pond
are a fictional world in which she finds
herself with a real face that exults:
"I know what young women know.
I will survive this sorrow. You will help."
I lay a fat broad hand into
your child's hand and was engulfed
as if I were the child and you

the swallowing father. "How long
have I been here?" asks White-eye
up from his dungeon, dazzled
in the courtyard, "Ten years? Twenty?"

The patient foreboding of the flesh
tells you nothing. You have been here
so long you want to die. The manacles
still bite. Neither of us holds this whip.

We are part of the crowd
that pokes around the market checking teeth,
biceps, hair, and one another
with the natural curiosity of lovers,

slaves, children, to discover
the one living thing
in there, moving
the giant figures through their roles.

The entire congregation of some exotic sect
of Hasidim takes over the airport. Everywhere
black overcoats and bright skullcaps run
for planes as if the game were over and the fans rush the field.
From each plane many famous rabbis disembark,
a committee of great teachers has arrived
from the air. The disciples circle them
and sing, some throw open their coats
in unthinkable abandon, some even their shirts,
they raise their arms—drumsticks that flap
in black sleeves, and beat against their chests
with a steady tempo forward: one red face
and curly beard flashes against the lattice
of the hangar wall with his mouth locked open.
They hand out bills with pictures of praying Jews.
They march the rabbis out into the night
with Bom Bu-Bu Bom-Bom, Bom-Bu-Bu Bom-Bom-Bom,
the bridegroom's song for the Sabbath Queen arriving.
I do not understand why my cheeks are wet,
and lean forward, choked, unable to laugh
even at myself deceived again
by a brotherhood I stand outside of.

The Morning Of Execution

A tree nubile with unripe plums
and a low bush with green hard
lemons darken the prison yard.
The morning mist has not yet
burned away and on the wires
the dew still shines. The silent visitors
reach small gifts through to me.
I turn from them and care only
for the windfall fruits, redlaced,
green and spotted in the trodden grass,
becoming soft jewels in the hand.
Cold and puzzled by this waste.

The Old Prince

>The slippage of style is so fast
the mothers of our archaic class
no longer know how to arrange
a marriage for their daughters.
They cast around for advice
and find that no one, noone knows.
The girls have their own uschooled will
and the men of the right families
behave like pigs. What shall they do
with their delightful Kitty? She is in love
with a series of unsuitable men:
a subterranean, a dancing doll,
an organist, a poet and an organ.
Marriage! Marriage! The smart talk
is of divorce. This is the nature
of the new age. Wife from husband,
shall from will. There is no change:
the virtuous have all the power
still, the sinners all the grace.

The Revolution Decides Not To Occur

She is so exotic, for relief I stare
out the window at the ocean
growing black. If I looked at her
steadily I would gape like a clown.

Her rapt smile as she plays her hair
before her face suggests some deep
sufficiency of knowledge. It is the queer
knowledge of Narcissus in his half sleep.

The conversation around her flies
swiftly and I notice her attention pass
through her hair to the thighs
that bulge her tenuous dress.

I become aware that she observes
my thighs but finally with boredom
returns to hers. This order preserves
its dreaming equilibrium.

Three Ring Circus

It begins in danger always, on the wire
the aerialist, with all breath around her
hung, dives and misses, no, catches the thin
bar and begins the slow triumphant arc
over our heads her heels over her head
in air spread eagled sailing free and coming in
fast with elephants, drums, trumpets entering
lunging and they catch breath again in the dark
back and shouts break—pennants, horns
and whistles and now, ah, the yes-yes clowns
wave and stamp in bloopy shoes and shriek,
howl, whoop and the whole tent balloons
with exploded breath and the aerialist flips
herself neat onto the elephant and marches
out standing, bowing, waving ostrich plumes,
the clowns disappear in giggles, a dog
rackets outside in the rain and you
push me off and close and roll away
keeping secret till you come again.

Time And The String Quartet Domesticate Eros

They are tempestuous in white ties,
black suits and gleaming shoes, seated.

And what proceeds from them in C
sharp minor surely is tempestuous.

It subverts all other order. Abandon
is delicious and to such

ecstatic stuff! It was arranged
to end. We turn, stand, bang

our knees against the seats, fumble
with our coats, remind ourselves

of home, return. We never once
dreamed of real submission.

Tired With The Hunt And Cold

Tired with the hunt and cold
I sat down to read
like an old scholarly mystic
the traditional text of the stream
crowded with life and fast
between its granite banks
of glacial residue.
The trout and crayfish hid
as if they filled my mind
but I was already flown
outward and inward at once
in a constant tumbling race
over the gravel and past
the man on the bank, breathless—
its motion my stillness.

What *Is* The Condition Of Music?

Music as Civic Order

Ringing the tables of the gaudy plaza
with heads together they buzz and they sway over
scores like forsythia in a strong wind.
Waving their arms and their hands
conducting the shapes out of air,
they weave in their frail steel chairs.
                        Busy.
They will never offend *il Principe*; easy
to govern. The Mayor is lazy, the sheriff
rocks his bulk back in his chair,
his raised feet dance in the air
a coda, a musical close.

Outlaw Music

Well, now that's over, the door
burst in, the wall split through which
the heavy breathers push to fill
the tight house with dancing, drowning
in the deaf-making music and belching
from the beer flowing from the stone prick
of a jubilant statue of Bacchus
and the girls forget themselves, skirts
above their breasts as they flash their white
unsunned asses and the house is all meat,
shrieks and hair, bracing body salts
and ecstasy with everything thrown back,
walls and heads, mouths and all throats
pouring full and lost in all that opening.

From The Marrano (1988)

The Kabalist

I have an indoor mind: a small room,
a focused light, many books
and one window shoulder height.
The only parts of nature known to me
are my wrists, hands and fingers:
they move, are warm, and change
too quickly for serious study.
From the window, a large world
full of rows of things: bushes,
trees, rivers, cows in line.
It is a boring text, this flat grid.
On my shelves, even the meanest book
retreats in depth and joins with all my books,
petals moving toward the fertile center,
and can place me back and back behind myself
reading the book behind the book, until
the blossom opens and we form one text,
one complete mind, the one order.

The Marrano

Art is a remedy for the worst diseases of the mind,
the corruption of consciousness.   R.G. Collingwood

God wants the souls of the faithful,
not their corpses. He has carrion enough.
In The Golem it explains
from moments of the highest danger
he saves us, always in the form of wonders,
like making a new man. For this truth
we struggle in disguise.
I moved to Hamburg or Seville, bought
a bakery or clothing store, a new name,
and lived openly, spoke like a native. I was
a kind of native, the most internal exile.
I could not change my name
because I was committed to disguise,
from Weiss to Scheiss, Hermano to Marrano.
I am his pig. To hide Him I renounce Him.
My teacher cared for me, a prize student.
To spare my feeling he asked me to leave the class
during his diatribes against the Jews.
I listened from the hallway, grateful
for this lesson in accommodation.
Modesty and secrecy are virtues of the chosen.
Study the pig for modesty. The cat
buries the emblem of the world. We learn
in secret through closed doors, all love.
I welcome the need to convert, create
an adequate corruption of the mind
fit for understanding, for the sacred,
the one text, the one ungainly text,
saying *Alles in ordnung ist*,
meaning another, unimaginable order.
The Gnostics were right, the world is made of shit.
I made my life a work of art expressing this.

A Librarian Of Alexandria

She has the manuscripts of Sappho in her hand,
the personal body, not a scribe's work
but shining with her mark, Sappho's, actual.
She seals this papyrus in its own urn.

This is before Actium. She knows
the line of fire of the Roman mind,
learned in her body's long analysis.

Homer's two books, Moses' five,
in their own hand, blotted and corrected,
Aeschylus and Sophocles, not one
play lost, and all of Euripides
on the stupidity of gods, and many voices
wholly lost to us whom the grammarians
did not quote nor the invaders preserve
as mementos of the Greek defeat.

She has buried them deep in her own earth:
the Psalms for preservation and Solomon's song.
She sways above them.

The books of the soul are dreaming underground
at their true depth, waiting to be found.
She has worked long at this, will defy
fire, time as fire, the fire in the mind,
using an Egyptian art. She has saved
all of Heraclitus, to mock him;
Aristophanes to make us sane;
of Archilochos the whole warm body.

In her white dress she is the one steady light
in the abandoned mine among the smoking lamps.
She preserves last

those that bear the stinging taste to the mouth
of love of tragedy—
          kneels as she buries them—

with her face lowered in the golden tent of her hair
that brushes the floor in a circle around her, she smells
her own spiced oils (that aromatic body
knows how the satyr plays)
          —all the Satyr Plays.

A Short Season In Hell
for Rimbaud

His face fills with a tormented red
as he fumbles the unknown language, words, sounds,
and in him swells the panic of a child
among staring strangers who refuse to understand.

Abandoned by language, her most complete dependent
who learned his world in her skirts, found his house,
his street, the body's smells and sounds and lines—
to feel, to eat—a world ending loss,

until to rescue him the two arrive—
his wife, his daughter, with deft waving of worlds
and shaping of sounds with swift fingers, expressive
precise words, the flood of comfort of words

in loved mouths, a corner of tooth, saliva
at lip, the crest and trough of a wave that carries
closer in flood in a boat filled with flowers,
him to himself, rising and falling through mist.

Still with a spyglass on shore he sits between them
and drinks a brandy. His daughter, with his face
on his mother's body, reaches for his arm
and covers him with her silver intelligence,

her generous laugh, and leans across to whisper
a joke to her mother who joins in chorus with her.
His wife leans against him—scented air,
rose, linden, white tobacco flower—

and the stranded one returns, touches her face,
having burned with the childlike terror of the dead
who hover among us to make the last revisions
unable to shape the words that must be said
before in the grass they assume their fixed positions.

After The Revolution

They both held their silence at separate windows
breathing so softly that the faint
rush of air would not interfere
with the fluting of the thrushes back and forth
across the four corners of the garden,
and savored together the lente, lente,
the darkening room, the bird song
in the middle distance and the crescent moon
rising. Their silence in this vigil was important.
His voice had grown mechanical
and oppressed him with his own spirit's death
laboring for a cause that changed and changed.
He was once so passionate in battle
and beautiful, Trotsky said his eyes alone
were revolution in the name of more perfect love.
That was the evening he disappeared.
She never knew when he left the room,
whether the Security Police arrived
and he went out to meet them, or merely walked
into something unofficial,
a new life or death in the newest order,
the moon behind a cloud, nothing and silence.

Coney Island Roller Coaster

On the Cyclone on a heavy-fleshed hot night
we chill ourselves in the wild rush of air—
with stopped hearts in the falls, and the slow climb to where
the dark ocean holds once, drops then from sight
as the heart stops again. Some ragged kids,
all under fifteen, on cue, at once,
climb out between the cars and balance
on them—hang on the outsides, each trick a bid
for glory: somersaults, handstands
in seats, leaps from car to car like trout
climbing white water, and as blind
to danger. Can I stop them? One lands
on me and vaults off. I'm afraid to reach out—
they are so sure of foot and hand and mind.
A Cretan bull dance, handstands on gilded horns
and ghostly, flashing discipline.
And I descend with my daughter who with fierce
crimped lips will not be afraid and my son
who screams with serene abandon and loves it and is.

Family Plot

I was a dutiful son to the end.
In the smallest lapse of duty
I dream of her frown of pain.
Now it has been ten years
since I have been to her grave.
Will I leave ten stones on her grave?
Then she can hold up her head
among the dead and we're back
in the old collaboration,
lying to the living,
the dutiful cousins who visit
among those obliterating
fixed waves of stone—
lying to the dead.

Great Horned Owl

On a dawn walk I startled
a great horned owl, wary,
near, on a low limb
of a tree downhill from me.
Those slow wings opened,
broad as a man, two men,
and he sank fast down
into the hillside in blank
silence, a wall toppling
its whole enormous length
that does not touch a thing.

Margaret Roper
after Holbein's drawing

To be the favorite daughter
of one like More imposes
with serene dangerous love
the curse of its obligations.
She knew her father well—
the peril of his laugh,
his last sticking point.
It made her face a dove
landing on a wire,
its white wings outspread
to drag against the wind,
her mouth the wire—
thin, wary, guarded.
She broke through the guard to More
on his last trip to the Tower
and kissed him again and again.
No one stopped her. He wrote
his last night in the Tower:
"I cumber you dear Margaret
very much....I never
liked your manner better
than when you kissed me last.
For I like when daughterly love
and dear charity
hath no leisure to look
to worldly courtesy."
Double: the gentle and ruthless
demand to protect the thing
he could no longer protect,
his head impaled on a spike
naked on London Bridge
and her last obligation—
to take it down and carry

the drained thing home
enclosed in rich cloths
and return it at last to his body.

Emily Dickinson's Room: Main Street, Amherst

Down through the cross of her windows
facing the West she saw
her father interpose
his hat, shoulders, shoes,
as he came or went or strolled
under the high limbed trees—
her shutters always open—
their silent, legible gestures
of intimate conversation,
one face obtruding, pressing,
one listening, looking down;
and the children crouch on the lawn
to watch the puppy squat;
and the cat brace its legs
into a panting scaffold
to hoist a stubborn mole.
To the south she saw the street
through two uncurtained windows:
the striking fellow in black
ministering to the dead
reel the thread of his rounds;
the fire volunteers
in ceremonious panic
clamor out to the farms;
the farmers ride their wagons
that screech under flax and corn
and roped by the neck behind
the doomed steer low
his way to the abattoir;
but mostly the garden change
from crocus to tulip to rose,
their cohorts dying in ranks
yet coming and coming again
till driven to sleep by snow
and locked into place by ice.

Poem Beginning With A Line By Hollis Frampton

        I
Lithic and late as all October dying,
sharing nothing, you dying

in silence to wall in your own fight
against death, stone by stone, your right

to a private death. You didn't want to waste
the dying year, weeks, days, in "the most

boring conversation in the world"
and so you chose covert action, curled

in upon yourself with drugs and work
to finish, and left us with an empty circle

of stunned phone calls and the obit in
the *Times*. I would have made your coffin

with my own hands, covered myself with dust,
some ritual for your death, something to grasp.

        II
Some ritual for your death, something to grasp,
a gathering for farewell of scholiasts

to catalogue your films, annote, compend,
cover and shade you with a pleach of friends

for finale to the throb and hum
of body and house around us in your ear.

You don't need to bear me working on
my problems with death. You the occasion.

A private death. I wanted to invade.
We were the same age. I had private ends—

to be free of the fear that truth blinds and kills.
Let truth have its own prurient way.

I can close my eyes, shut out obtruding light
and late in the dying year can open them.

Puppet Theater

Unfolding from his box,
His hollow wooden head
So delicately carved
And loose on its silken thread

Holds one complete idea:
That motion from the soul,
Any inward motion,
Is waste and uncontrol.

Actors work their lines,
Root in themselves to find
Possession, rage, etcetera—
Half understood and blind—

But the hand outspread above,
With a jerk, twist or nod,
Can sweep the surrendered limbs
To be wild and obscene as a god.

Tarzan & Co.

I lived in the caress
of the most dangerous
wolves, apes, big cats,
knowing them in my hands,
the thick ruff at the throat,
the soft skin of the belly,
the vulnerable crotch
and their rich Edwardian speech,
taking on their powers
with their fearsome tenderness
like the English nobleman
who turned toward savageness
against the systematic
savage trade at home.
This was after the war
after the famous photos
of death camps and the entrance
of the new word "genocide"—
our apartment overcrowded
with Jewish refugees
sleeping on the floor.
Growing away from childhood
I turned for my defense
to a sterner animal code,
more instinctive, perilous,
than the mild rational world
of my accommodating home.
Sometimes I would stand
at the corner for an hour
buried in my book
until some thoughtful neighbor
would grab me by the elbow
to steer me across the street
still absent in the dream

of an animal poise of body,
faster, more alert,
enough to seize the cobra
arched and ready to strike,
to save the young, swimming,
with a knife across the belly
of the perilous crocodile,
and knowing a hidden language
that I had been denied,
the message of the spoor,
the turn of twig and vine.
This was the dream of knowledge
I returned from as a beast
to change the world to beasts.

The Drawing Of Thomas Wyatt By Holbein
"seme as you are" Wyatt to his son

I expected something softer than this stern
wary face—a full mouth, eyes
large and shadowed with a power less
manly. The drooping feathers, bird cries,

the seduction of the poems—all denied.
The mournful elegance, the songs of pain
were his public mask for real pain, the wounds
worn in translation. Only the scars remain

(that mouth!) to make the face—hanging beef
to serve a murderous king—witness
to the execution of friends on the blood-slick top.
All the power was wrong. His old mistress

Anne Boleyn had the soft mouth that betrays.
"Want nothing soft," mutters this face.

The Dybbuk

Sick with fearing to need you and my last refusal,
I watched the house across the way, the late night
scattering of lit windows—tall stairwells
descending in the fog as columns of light.
Then all went dark as mine, power failed,
my radio stopped its throbbing of Ravel.
I heard a window crank open wide
into the September chill, and a rough call
from someone unheard.   Then I stood inside
their room. They crowded me, touched my face:
I saw myself as many, then as one
trembling before me, cupped hands raised,
eyes lowered, offering—not from obligation
but wholly—then the swift inhabitation.

Then back in my room I watch the lights return
at window and stairwell, hear Ravel resume,
and see you toss in bed with sleep-heat, murmur
something indistinct—my old name.
Now the shock of double vision, its perpetual
astonishment beginning as I sit
beside you and watch you turn through new eyes
that want what I do not want, and do it.
Not from over my shoulder but from within
I see myself and myself fully replaced
lift the sheet and drive for something human,
some spirit that had died come to live
in me and offer me, that loved you in the past.
I see myself with horror give and give.

The Religion Of Art: 1 Feb 58

No one more remote than us
at twenty. I seem doll small
in memory: the lens long focus—
a tiny man, a tiny hospital.

When I left you on your high bed
you were white—a porcelain flask.
Our new son was bright red
and puckered like a dragon mask.

For a full day we timed contractions,
you dozed, I read aloud to you
how son kills father, father son,
in *Don Juan* by Victor Hugo.

The Don, while canonized at Mass,
wrings off his head in his high coffin,
flings it and kills the spiteful priest.
Better a devil of liberation

Then be a saint. You were being natural
until delivery and gas.
It was a simple country hospital,
no nursery, no wall of glass.

I got to see you, stunned face
to face with Matthew in your arms.
You were so addled with the nurse
you forgot my name for the state forms.

I too was dazed, so mastered by what
I thought I should feel, I never knew
what I felt—desperate
to kneel, to celebrate with you.

But I could never really force my breath
to thank for this single time he skipped
us, the child-killing Angel of Death
who delivered us bathed in blood from Egypt.

It's what I thought was due, to buy
my son from death. I had the rite wrong.
I only had to claim him from the rabbi
(who never had him) for a song.
A tiny refusal. Your time was full.
My mind reeked with the need for prayer.
In the religion of the Great Dispersal
my shul was the record player

turning the world on auto-repeat
eight times, before I could find
the firmness of Bach's first Cello Suite—
how adequate that sculpting of my mind.

The String Quartet

The first violinist, all of him, follows his arm,
his feet sway around him to keep him in balance
as he sways and lunges into the sounds he makes.
This is dance making music of the body.

The face of the second violinist is Unending Passion.
Such expressiveness, such deep response, would rouse
to sexual frenzy the weathered statues of the female saints.
His is the face of music as romance.

The cellist grinds his teeth, clenches his face in spasms
of control to keep down the groan, the song, the wild
lament he lets his bow alone sound across the strings.
His is the grimace of dignified loss in the tragic agon.

The violist sits and plays. Staid. In his face
the years in Brussels, tutelage at the old Conservatoire,
grubbing for meals, going back for practice, practice.
This is music itself as it leaves the body behind.

The Toy

Look at him circle (his key
unwinding behind his back)
the woman with outstretched arms—
the gentleman in black

who shrinks when we laugh at his fervent
celebration of life,
bowing at the waist
his glossy back to his wife,

to—imagine what you want—
a Minister of State,
a grande dame on her rounds,
the Poet Laureate,

a whore in a doorway slouched
and elaborately bored,
or portly kapos and bankers
swaggering abroad.

To all that appear, he bows
and his hat brushes his feet
with the calamitous respect
he's compelled to repeat and repeat.

Imagine him falling in love
with one who sings from her window:
unable to stop and smile
he sickens at each bow

as the central Mother of Sorrows
with a club in her outstretched hands
cries and demands that he stop
and he starts to puke as he bends.

Aristotle says
the comic figures we love
are smaller than life and shrink
as we laugh and loom above.

By now he can barely be seen,
our laughter has made him so small
he slips through the tight floorboards,
through layers of floors to fall

and fall to where we no longer
can see but still one hears
from deep beneath the foundation
the intimate howl of his gears.

The Via Negativa, Ojai, California

What could I have found to love in him,
this driving, bright-eyed priest of quietness,
a moonflower, a hanging fritillary,
asway in frail transparency?
And Krishnamurti said, "The truth can not
be repeated." Long pause. A meadowlark
resumed its complex, two-throated cycle of song,
the sound of audience murmur, bustle, breath,
the monotonous squawk of a baby. I in silence
trying to instruct my heart—in purity—
in my tight essential style. It was logic I loved.
I dreamed of the inward order that would rule
with *laissez faire*, with an invisible hand
the universal primal state of soul.
And he said again, "The truth can not be
repeated," and I tried to be free of my heart.

For Hollis Frampton (d. 1984)

You were always your own creation, Great Pretender.
How else understand yourself?

Well before you died you fit together
what you needed to do, and did, and with open hand

threw out the rest. I'm glad it bored you first
though I was still enchanted

with what you thought you knew, *Polumetis*.
I had vague boundaries too.

Two by Kurosawa and two six-packs each
and you taught me how to be a Samurai swordsman

swinging your tripod at Kings Highway Station
at dawn without staggering once—sure feet—

one with the virtuosi against defeat
in a defiantly archaic art.

You made film archaic—Oh the wonder
of lemon, the motion of it, still, light's

love of its engorged pores, its lemon color,
and the curl of darkness around it as the camera

turned, before story banished vision.
What I learned to see, preceptor.

Rachel cried when you died: "He was so vivid!"
I sank my head on my arms two nights running

drinking myself down. Again, but this time
with silence, you drank me flat on the table

and I prayed for the same house in hell
with you: and after that much work.

U.S. Signal Corps Footage

The sun went down for hours on Silver Lake
through low clouds and the sun path on the water
stretched over the whole end, catching the red
and spattering it down into the small waves
the breeze made and into the wake of motor boats,
a broad slash of light that spread and spread.
Suddenly each light-holding ripple
became a man, a captured army rose
to the tormented surface, thousands
of prisoners when we weren't taking prisoners
on a beach in the Pacific. Our machine guns
opened on them and they fell in waves
turning the ocean red and the camera ran and ran.
I could not stop, escape. The Signal Corps
records, insists, hides and protects this film,
forced me through the bone sockets
of its theater for cleared eyes: Immerse,
it says, bring it back, keep it, absorb.

To All The Gods At Once: A Prayer For Mercy

Those immediately around me, those in range of my voice, *eleison*

Those within line of sight, within reach, within the vibrating aura of smell, *eleison*

Those who see me stumbling up the stoop fumbling for my keys, *eleison*

Those with me who are also stupefied by drink in honor of Dionysius and Jack and Paul and Rosie, *eleison*

The queen of the incestuous elite in a small Midwestern capitol who is leaning against the refrigerator, the print of whose dress swirls down to a great circle on her left buttock, *eleison*

The unaccustomed half-nudes on the beach speaking Swedish, Finnish, Japanese, Basque, Dutch and Cree, *eleison*

The young sportswoman smelling richly of peach soap and horse shit, *eleison*

You, whose long breath and light snore carry me down to a child's obliterating sleep, *eleison*

You who believe that "Thought's the slave of life," *eleison*

Those who must know everything and explain everything, the coffee, the iced water, *eleison*

Those who insist on being understood perfectly, a hallucination of clarity in your sad, steady eyes, *eleison*

Those who make the unspeakable chatty, *eleison*

The Unmoved Mover, with her eyes moving in their stillness, and her mobile mouth, image of terror, who moves me and is unmoved, *eleison*

She who arrived and said that she was God's only daughter come to redeem the world—I was amused at first but then got angry and clomped out and bought the next morning's *Times* on my way home, which always feels like cheating, *eleison*

You who believe that "Life's the slave of thought," *eleison*

The quail who said, when it stunned itself on the plate glass, "It's not in nature," *eleison*

The wrong kind of fool when foolishness is the best guide, *eleison*

The one who said, "I am sensitive to multitudes," *eleison*

Those who, when the hundred flowers bloomed, confessed to the ten thousand things, became martyrs and officeholders in the next regime,

and him, who on a dig, discovered the ancient texts, gradually became dismayed at their sinister rectitude and destroyed them, was excommunicated by the Eternal Church and became the Messiah of the next one, *eleison*

You, doubtful yet serene, suave yet full of majesty, witty yet serious, who smiles and is vulnerable, *eleison*

You who believe that "Nature loves to hide," *eleison*

Beatrice the Partisan who led me from the perilous
    Upper City down through the sewers to the safety of
    an underground cell populated by all the noisy demons,
    eleison

You who will build a gazebo and a bed for the copulation of
    lovers above my grave, *eleison*

You whose face and body are smiling with inwardness,
    accomplished in all its lines, painted by Rembrandt with
    gold and shit, *eleison*

The oboist dozing in the pit while *Così* glitters above him
    with its fervent reeducation of instinct, *eleison*

The face on the medallion turned away, *eleison*

You who believe that "Nature hides to love," *eleison*

Dance Music

Dance Music

I hear the hum of the body
perfectly still, the ear
pressed to the door jamb, buzzing,
the whisper of breath in the nose,
a distant voice that calls,
the knock and swoosh of plumbing
rising and falling through walls,
the thump of the heart, the slight
shake of the frame at the stroke,
the refrigerator gurgling
and grumbling tirelessly,
while I hold myself deathly still,
absent from house and body
and the music persists in its motions.

One dim bulb
in cheap fluted glass
a half flight above
and a presence very close
that climbs in step with me.
What kind of Judge is he?
I know that flat face
and shark's flat eye,
the smooth breath in the climb
and the effortless moves behind
as if he understood
all that sharked through my mind.
—You, are you kind? I know
with your steel rasp skin
and sudden irresistible plunge
and your glass eye grin—
*You think what I really think,
grasp at the skull and dive.*

This is the year that death
robed in shit and sable
finds the key to the door
and lays himself down on our table
then gleams and clicks and hums
all night while the wind drones,
or sits in the oak chair
and watches us flinch and veer
away from his part of the room
and his voice booms in our ears
and his snake eye stare
then both of us play possum,
cold, unresponsive, dumb,
while we plot our escape from here.
We are dead already, go home!

We separate in heat—not another
body sweating, another cold mind
grasping for warmth: all longing denied
to keep the mind clean at the work of ending,
having room for no attachment further.
You and the vague women pressing in dreams
I push away, for the sake of the housefly
shuffling on my arm, his house soon
when he lays maggots under the skin
and drives me to greater removal from myself,
the feeling for what is: nature persistent
and self-absorbed, making my mind its mirror.
You lean on your elbow with a smile
that in this climate is intolerable.

The blossoms compete for the bee,
the apple, plum, cherry,

require its provident yearning,
its hairy legs, its probe,
even the useless hawthorn,
flowering to mock us and sting,
blossoming, blossoming.

Et in arcadia ego

As I stepped out of the car
before I reached the foggy
yellow globe of porchlight
I heard a low growl,
confident in menace,
a crash of brush, the scream
of a hare in three breaths
that stretched itself on the air
its intense high-pitched length
until a neck broke
and the bobcat bore away
through whispering uncut hay,
the grass the flesh is like,
the flesh that's like the grass.

Bathsheba

is now mature in creases, at ease
in shade as she bathes her quilted body. The light
is all in her face and it falls like death on skin.
Her smile is inward. The watcher hidden in night—
the king who eyes her from his roof, must murder
her husband first. Why does he love her? His sight
is inward too. He loves her. He'll get her.

It is May 15th, the air
outside the house is now
in harmony with air
within. How equable,
how utterly without
boundary it feels, to douse
all the lights and walk
in a starless, moonless night,
the house empty of me
and empty. Dangerous,
this small experiment—
abandon to senseless trust
with no inside or out
and no visible space.
I like it all too much.

She is buttoned to the throat
with a white, formal yoke.

The massive shutters are open
and fastened to the wall,

espaliers surround them
hung with pears and plums.

She leans from the dark room
into the welcoming air

and showers the street with the light
of her gap-toothed naked smile.

The borders in borders keep
this human explosion contained.

When Sappho says *asleep against the breast
of a friend* the breast is youthful, tender,
will not be pressed without a sudden moan
of dumbfounding pain, and the head that would rest
like air, like stone.

The Bat

On the stump of a torn wing
it planted itself in the driveway
and screeched to keep me away
from doing the merciful thing
and crushing it under my foot.
I scooped it up in my cap
and hid it away in a yew
to save it from the cat.
It would starve in a day or two.
I once heard a chipmunk scream
for hours in the slow jaws
of a king snake under the porch,
but the human terrified dream
in the beast face of that thing
made me unable to kill
as it lingered in suffering.
Don't test me on anything close.

"*Anyone incapable of deceit is incapable
of love.*" Stendhal

I was brought there to be read: the message
in the blank wall waiting to be called
into you, sweating on a sheet,
a string of twigs with a familiar face.
My mother, always steady, brushed your hair

and tied it with a red bow. You saw
my face and tried a feeble lie as I did:
a clench of mind, my coached face unmasked
smiling in terror. You asked for me
knowing you could read in my deceit,
brutal and incapable, the necessary fact.

The summer that their daughter Rachel (named
after my shining daughter) died
I paid the stiff visit to the house.
Her toys and flip-flops, all the plastic colors
were scattered around the lush uncut lawn
and piled on the porch, lights in dark places,
as if she still were balancing the sphere,
of herself unbroken, her rule.
I felt the need to gather things, but all
I touched would stick to my hand in shrill silence:
dolls' clothes, a yellow plastic bowl,
shoes, magic marker, bubble wand.

I am no longer the child slashed by wire
who snaked back into the locked city
to warn Jews of the plan, the unsealing
of sealed trains, how they were killed, the camps,
the doctor-judge selecting who will die
with the flick of his white baton on the railway siding.
I screamed, *Escape! Escape!* until
my throat closed, they thought me mad from loss,
everybody's loss, and brought me bread
to stop my raving—later seized by Germans
and pushed through all I had seen before, then killed.
Today I am a man in this dream
of new terror with a man's grave face
and they believe me they must kill to live.

When staring at the lake I died.
The blinding, light-scattering crushed
foil surface barrier to vision
vanished and I saw clear to the bottom—
the water was brilliant air. On boulders
come to light in that buried world,
stood my parents, aunts and uncles,
many friends, waving their welcome to me
who now at last could see.

from East Long Pond

Immersion

When I drop the bar of forced
inattention that scatters
me all around the house
it is easy to lose myself—
music can claim me entirely
from clamoring me! me! me!

It is hard to attend to the lives
singing around me: frogs,
flies, leaves, birds,
woof of bear or owl
rolling across the lake
and the trill and howl of the loon.
Always a noise in my head—
the din of my body moving
my laboring, reeling breath
deafen and enclose
my mind in a sensible cloud
of everything it knows
except for the voice that calls:
"Stop, stop, stop
this busy chatter and roar
and sit and be still and hear."

The lake is cold in its season.
A mist squats and is still
over water, recently ice,
and the rising sun makes it glow,
a fire in a field of snow,
before it breathes it in
and leaves the mirror clear.
My daughter's afraid I will fall

out of my light canoe
in this icy water and die.
She knows there is something to fear:
even in midsummer heat
the thrill of danger swimming
on the warm surface above
the scrotum-and-nipple-tightening
depth of this bottomless lake
and the danger of the claim
its beauty makes on me.

Garish and magnanimous,
the sun descended in fire
in the whole western sky,
and the long sloping shoulders
of Monadnock and her clouds
diminished with distance
in my rear view mirror
until I saw entire
the profile of the mountain,
its black animal spine
against the lurid sky.

I needed the full view
and climbed out of the car
to see it face to face
then distance vanished inside me--
without moving at all
I was suddenly crouched on its flank
and buried my face in the leafmold,
sweet-smelling, delicate, moist,
my cheeks brushed by ferns,
and the outspread mass of the mountain,
embraced me as I shivered
in the cold, early spring,

cliffs, streams, falls,
boulders, trees, snow.

Crunching under our sandals tiny snails,
so frail, even to brush them kills them.
We stop--with no place to set our feet.

I can't find the road
that curves into the woods
then into a dappled clearing,
the way to the red house
surrounded by four trees
between two ponds,
one large, one small,
and the music of their short
waterfalls and graceful
inner light with large
windows, rooms, and broad,
high hall. Now,
walking into town
to buy the *Times* the long,
early morning shadow
walking before me and sleep
still glazing my eyes I struggle
to separate the loss
of a real home from a dream
home and I can barely push
my shoulders through
the battering wall of air—
this too is dream.

Years ago, a long search through my house
for *Les fleurs du mal*, every room, the attic,

then later in a village where I knew
I could be myself without restraint, because
everyone knew everyone and everyone saw
all the enterings, withdrawals, visits by day or night,
I looked in the library and bookstore in vain
for an Italian dictionary to lead me
through a love poem--naked or veiled
in half-alien sounds by Montale I needed
to understand and could not.
This happened often, and I found myself
leaning against the wall of a house that shrank
to my size, then smaller, then me like a tiny ant
that walked the full length and back of every needle
of a spruce I studied closely for many days.

Counting breaths, my heartbeats, paces to the door,
feet in a line of verse, quartets, cantatas,
blows of the hammer, turns of the wrench and screw,
steps on stairs up to the next floor,
seconds it takes for the high wisp of cloud
to vapor away in sun,
even as I pull my body through water
swimming, counting strokes in the glacial lake
and laps in the tedious, eye-stinging pool,
this minimal ordering of the world
lulls and steadies the mind's loose barrel
rolling thunder slamming below-decks against
the bone hull of the storm-tumbling ship.

Who we were last spring, whose thigh
and whose mouth was opening and hands flowed,
we could not separate. You, opening your eyes,
slowly, taking hours, brown, with clear lines,

before I tumbled into them, I seem
to remember, though I cannot tell you
whether early or late.

It is winter now. Waking in our deep
bed under heavy blankets, the room crowded
with ghosts, whispering their terrible message,
that no one we love will ever be forgotten,
and seal us in archaic dreams of love--
Mother, Carlo, Deborah, Alice, Dan.

Curled tight around my wife
from the pulse in my face, across
the stubble field of my torso,
my happy prick asleep,
down to my cool feet,
everything touching at once
the skin and the heft behind it
and the shifting passage of breath.
How confusing the boundary of body!
In this confusion, delight.

Douglas Kinsey is a painter and monotyper. He has exhibited throughout this country as well as in England, Sweden and Japan. His illustrations have mostly been for books of poetry. For twelve years he has been a Professor Emeritus at the University of Notre Dame, but early on he taught in the University of North Dakota as well as in the colleges of Berea and Oberlin. He is also a musician who plays early music.

Fomite
Burlington, VT

A fomite is a medium capable of transmitting infectious organisms from one individual to another.

"The activity of art is based on the capacity of people to be infected by the feelings of others." Tolstoy, *What Is Art?*

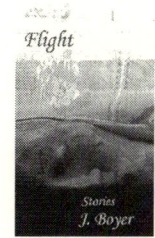

Flight and Other Stories - Jay Boyer

In *Flight and Other Stories,* we're with the fattest woman on earth as she draws her last breaths and her soul ascends toward its final reward. We meet a divorcee who can fly with no more effort than flapping her arms. We follow a middle-aged butler whose love affair with a young woman leads him first to the mysteries of bondage and then to the pleasures of malice. Story by story, we set foot into worlds so strange as to seem all but surreal, yet everything feels familiar, each moment rings true. And that's when we recognize we're in the hands of one of America's truly original talents.

Loisaida - Dan Chodorokoff

Catherine, a young anarchist estranged from her parents and squatting in an abandoned building on New York's Lower East Side, is fighting with her boyfriend and conflicted about her work on an underground newspaper. After learning of a developer's plans to demolish a community garden, Catherine builds an alliance with a group of Puerto Rican community activists. Together they confront the confluence of politics, money, and real estate that rule Manhattan. All the while she learns important lessons from her great-grandmother's life in the Yiddish anarchist movement that flourished on the Lower East Side at the turn of the century. In this coming-of-age story, family saga, and tale of urban politics, Dan Chodorkoff explores the "principle of hope" and examines how memory and imagination inform social change.

Improvisational Arguments - Anna Faktorovich

Improvisational Arguments is written in free verse to capture the essence of modern problems and triumphs. The poems clearly relate short, frequently humorous, and occasionally tragic stories about travels to exotic and unusual places, fantastic realms, abnormal jobs, artistic innovations, political objections, and misadventures with love.

Carts and Other Stories - Zdravka Evtimova

Roots and wings are the key words that best describe the short story collection *Carts and Other Stories,* by Zdravka Evtimova. The book is emotionally multilayered and memorable because of its internal power, vitality and ability to touch both your heart and your mind. Within its pages, the reader discovers new perspectives and true wealth, and learns to see the world with different eyes. The collection lives on the borders of different cultures. *Carts and Other Stories* will take the reader to wild and powerful Bulgarian mountains, to silver rains in Brussels, to German quiet winter streets, and to wind-bitten crags in Afghanistan.

This book lives for those seeking to discover the beauty of the world around them, and will have them appreciating what they have—and perhaps what they have lost as well.

Fomite
Burlington, VT

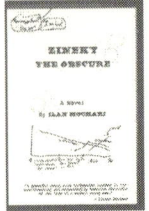

Zinsky the Obscure - Ilan Mochari

"If your childhood is brutal, your adulthood becomes a daily attempt to recover: a quest for ecstasy and stability in recompense for their early absence." So states the 30-year-old Ariel Zinsky, whose bachelor-like lifestyle belies the torturous youth he is still coming to grips with. As a boy, he struggles with the beatings themselves; as a grownup, he struggles with the world's indifference to them. *Zinsky the Obscure* is his life story, a humorous chronicle of his search for a redemptive ecstasy through sex, an entrepreneurial sports obsession, and finally, the cathartic exercise of writing it all down. Fervently recounting both the comic delights and the frightening horrors of a life in which he feels—always—that he is not like all the rest, Zinsky survives the worst and relishes the best with idiosyncratic style, as his heartbreak turns into self-awareness and his suicidal ideation into self-regard. A vivid evocation of the all-consuming nature of lust and ambition—and the forces that drive them.

Kasper Planet: Comix and Tragix - Peter Schumann

The British call him Punch; the Italians, Pulchinella; the Russians, Petruchka; the Native Americans, Coyote. These are the figures we may know. But every culture that worships authority will breed a Punch-like, anti-authoritarian resister. Yin and yang—it has to happen. The Germans call him Kasper. Truth-telling and serious pranking are dangerous professions when going up against power. Bradley Manning sits naked in solitary; Julian Assange is pursued by Interpol, Obama's Department of Justice, and Amazon.com. But—in contrast to merely human faces—masks and theater can often slip through the bars. Consider our American Kaspers: Charlie Chaplin, Woody Guthrie, Abby Hoffman, the Yes Men—theater people all, utilizing various forms to seed critique. Their profiles and tactics have evolved along with those of their enemies. Who are the bad guys that call forth the Kaspers? Over the last half century, with his Bread & Puppet Theater, Peter Schumann has been tireless in naming them, excoriating them with Kasperdom....*from Marc Estrin's Foreword to Planet Kasper*

The Co-Conspirator's Tale - Ron Jacobs

There's a place where love and mistrust are never at peace; where duplicity and deceit are the universal currency. *The Co-Conspirator's Tale* takes place within this nebulous firmament. There are crimes committed by the police in the name of the law. Excess in the name of revolution. The combination leaves death in its wake and the survivors struggling to find justice in a San Francisco Bay Area noir by the author of the underground classic *The Way the Wind Blew: A History of the Weather Underground* and the novel *Short Order Frame Up*.

All the Sinners Saints - Ron Jacobs

A young draftee named Victor Willard goes AWOL in Germany after an altercation with a commanding officer. Porgy is an African-American GI involved with the international Black Panthers and German radicals. Victor and a female radical named Ana fall in love. They move into Ana's room in a squatted building near the US base in Frankfurt. The international campaign to free Black revolutionary Angela Davis is coming to Frankfurt. Porgy and Ana are key organizers and Victor spends his days and nights selling and smoking hashish, while becoming addicted to heroin. Police and narcotics agents are keeping tabs on them all. Politics, love, and drugs. Truths, lies, and rock and roll. *All the Sinners Saints* is a story of people seeking redemption in a world awash in sin.

Fomite
Burlington, VT

Short Order Frame Up - Ron Jacobs

1975. America as lost its war in Vietnam and Cambodia. Racially tinged riots are tearing the city of Boston apart. The politics and counterculture of the 1960s are disintegrating into nothing more than sex, drugs, and rock and roll. The Boston Red Sox are on one of their improbable runs toward a postseason appearance. In a suburban town in Maryland, a young couple are murdered and another young man is accused. The couple are white and the accused is black. It is up to his friends and family to prove he is innocent. This is a story of suburban ennui, race, murder, and injustice. Religion and politics, liberal lawyers and racist cops. In *Short Order Frame Up*, Ron Jacobs has written a piece of crime fiction that exposes the wound that is US racism. Two cultures existing side by side and across generations--a river very few dare to cross. His characters work and live with and next to each other, often unaware of each other's real life. When the murder occurs, however, those people that care about the man charged must cross that river and meet somewhere in between in order to free him from (what is to them) an obvious miscarriage of justice.

Loosestrife - Greg Delanty

This book is a chronicle of complicity in our modern lives, a witnessing of war and the destruction of our planet. It is also an attempt to adjust the more destructive blueprint myths of our society. Often our cultural memory tells us to keep quiet about the aspects that are most challenging to our ethics, to forget the violations we feel and tremors that keep us distant and numb.

When You Remember Deir Yassin - R. L. Green

When You Remember Deir Yassin is a collection of poems by R. L. Green, an American Jewish writer, on the subject of the occupation and destruction of Palestine. Green comments: "Outspoken Jewish critics of Israeli crimes against humanity have, strangely, been called 'anti-Semitic' as well as the hilariously illogical epithet 'self-hating Jews.' As a Jewish critic of the Israeli government, I have come to accept these accusations as a stamp of approval and a badge of honor, signifying my own fealty to a central element of Jewish identity and ethics: one must be a lover of truth and a friend to the oppressed, and stand with the victims of tyranny, not with the tyrants, despite tribal loyalty or self-advancement. These poems were written as expressions of outrage, and of grief, and to encourage my sisters and brothers of every cultural or national grouping to speak out against injustice, to try to save Palestine, and in so doing, to reclaim for myself my own place as part of the Jewish people." Poems in the original English are accompanied by Arabic translations.

Roadworthy Creature, Roadworthy Craft - Kate Magill

Words fail but the voice struggles on. The culmination of a decade's worth of performance poetry, *Roadworthy Creature, Roadworthy Craft* is Kate Magill's first full-length publication. In lines that are sinewy yet delicate, Magill's poems explore the terrain where idea and action meet, where bodies and words commingle to form a strange new flesh, a breathing text, an "I" that spirals outward from itself.

Fomite
Burlington, VT

Visiting Hours - Jennifer Anne Moses
Visiting Hours, a novel-in-stories, explores the lives of people not normally met on the page—-AIDS patients and those who care for them. Set in Baton Rouge, Louisiana, and written with large and frequent dollops of humor, the book is a profound meditation on faith and love in the face of illness and poverty.

The Listener Aspires to the Condition of Music - Barry Goldensohn
"I know of no other selected poems that selects on one theme, but this one does, charting Goldensohn's career-long attraction to music's performance, consolations and its august, thrilling, scary and clownish charms. Does all art aspire to the condition of music as Pater claimed, exhaling in a swoon toward that one class act? Goldensohn is more aware than the late 19th century of the overtones of such breathing: his poems thoroughly round out those overtones in a poet's lifetime of listening."
John Peck, poet, editor, Fellow of the American Academy of Rome

The Derivation of Cowboys & Indians - Joseph D. Reich
The Derivation of Cowboys & Indians represents a profound journey, a breakdown of the American Dream from a social, cultural, historical, and spiritual point of view. Reich examines in concise detail the loss of the collective unconscious, commenting on our contemporary postmodern culture with its self-interested excesses, on where and how things all go wrong, and how social/political practice rarely meets its original proclamations and promises. Reich's surreal and self-effacing satire brings this troubling message home. *The Derivation of Cowboys & Indians* is a desperate search and struggle for America's literal, symbolic, and spiritual home.

Views Cost Extra - L.E. Smith
Views that inspire, that calm, or that terrify—all come at some cost to the viewer. In *Views Cost Extra* you will find a New Jersey high school preppy who wants to inhabit the "perfect" cowboy movie, a rural mailman disgusted with the residents of his town who wants to live with the penguins, an ailing screen-writer who strikes a deal with Johnny Cash to reverse an old man's failures, an old man who ponders a young man's suicide attempt, a one-armed blind blues singer who wants to reunite with the car that took her arm on the assembly line— and more. These stories suggest that we must pay something to live even ordinary lives.

Entanglements - Tony Magistrale
A poet and a painter may employ different mediums to express the same snow-blown afternoon in January, but sometimes they find a way to capture the moment in such a way that their respective visions still manage to stir a reverberation, a connection. In part, that's what *Entanglements* seeks to do. Not so much for the poems and paintings to speak directly to one another, but for them to stir points of similarity.

Fomite
Burlington, VT

Travers' Inferno - L.E. Smith

In the 1970's, churches began to burn in Burlington, Vermont. If it was arson, no one or no reason could be found to blame. This book suggests arson, but makes no claim to historical realism. It claims, instead, to capture the dizzying 70's zeitgeist of aggressive utopian movements, distrust in authority, escapist alternative lifestyles, and a bewildered society of onlookers. In the tradition of John Gardner's *Sunlight Dialogues*, the characters of *Travers' Inferno* are colorful and damaged, sometimes comical, sometimes tragic, looking for meaning through desperate acts. Travers Jones, the protagonist, is grounded in the transcendent—philosophy, epilepsy, arson as purification—and mystified by the opposite sex, haunted by an absent father and directed by an uncle with a grudge. He is seduced by a professor's wife and chased by an endearing if ineffective sergeant of police. There are secessionist Quebecois involved in these church burns who are murdering as well as pilfering and burning. There are changing alliances, violent deaths, lovemaking, and a belligerent cat.

The Empty Notebook Interrogates Itself - Susan Thomas

The Empty Notebook began its life as a very literal metaphor for a few weeks of what the poet thought was writer's block, but was really the struggle of an eccentric persona to take over her working life. It won. And for the next three years everything she wrote came to her in the voice of the Empty Notebook, who, as the notebook began to fill itself, became rather opinionated, changed gender, alternately acted as bully and victim, had many bizarre adventures in exotic locales, and developed a somewhat politically incorrect attitude. It then began to steal the voices and forms of other poets and tried to immortalize itself in various poetry reviews. It is now thrilled to collect itself in one slim volume.

My God, What Have We Done? - Susan Weiss

In a world afflicted with war, toxicity, and hunger, does what we do in our private lives really matter? Fifty years after the creation of the atomic bomb at Los Alamos, newlyweds Pauline and Clifford visit that once-secret city on their honeymoon, compelled by Pauline's fascination with Oppenheimer, the soulful scientist. The two stories emerging from this visit reverberate back and forth between the loneliness of a new mother at home in Boston and the isolation of an entire community dedicated to the development of the bomb. While Pauline struggles with unforeseen challenges of family life, Oppenheimer and his crew reckon with forces beyond all imagining. Finally the years of frantic research on the bomb culminate in a stunning test explosion that echoes a rupture in the couple's marriage. Against the backdrop of a civilization that's out of control, Pauline begins to understand the complex, potentially explosive physics of personal relationships. At once funny and dead serious, *My God, What Have We Done?* sifts through the ruins left by the bomb in search of a more worthy human achievement.

Suite for Three Voices - Derek Furr

Suite for Three Voices is a dance of prose genres, teeming with intense human life in all its humor and sorrow. A son uncovers the horrors of his father's wartime experience, a hitchhiker in a muumuu guards a mysterious parcel, a young man foresees his brother's brush with death on September 11. A Victorian poetess encounters space aliens and digital archives, a runner hears the voice of a dead friend in the song of an indigo bunting, a teacher seeks wisdom from his students' errors and Neil Young. By frozen waterfalls and neglected graveyards, along highways at noon and rivers at dusk, in the sound of bluegrass, Beethoven, and Emily Dickinson, the essays and fiction in this collection offer moments of vision.

Fomite
Burlington, VT

As It Is On Earth - Peter M. Wheelwright

Four centuries after the Reformation Pilgrims sailed up the down-flowing watersheds of New England, Taylor Thatcher, irreverent scion of a fallen family of Maine Puritans, is still caught in the turbulence. In his errant attempts to escape from history, the young college professor is further unsettled by his growing attraction to Israeli student Miryam Bluehm as he is swept by Time through the "family thing"—from the tangled genetic and religious history of his New England parents to the redemptive birthday secret of Esther Fleur Noire Bishop, the Cajun-Passamaquoddy woman who raised him and his younger half-cousin/half-brother, Bingham. The landscapes, rivers, and tidal estuaries of Old New England and the Mayan Yucatan are also casualties of history in Thatcher's story of Deep Time and re-discovery of family on Columbus Day at a high-stakes gambling casino, rising in resurrection over the starlit bones of a once-vanquished Pequot Indian tribe.

Love's Labours - Jack Pulaski

In the four stories and two novellas that comprise *Love's Labors* the protagonists, Ben and Laura, discover in their fervid romance and long marriage their interlocking fates, and the histories that preceded their births. They also learned something of the paradox between love and all the things it brings to its beneficiaries: bliss, disaster, duty, tragedy, comedy, the grotesque, and tenderness. Ben and Laura's story is also the particularly American tale of immigration to a new world. Laura's story begins in Puerto Rico, and Ben's lineage is Russian-Jewish. They meet in City College of New York, a place at least analogous to a melting pot. Laura struggles to rescue her brother from gang life and heroin. She is mother to her younger sister; their mother Consuelo is the financial mainstay of the family and consumed by work. Despite filial obligations, Laura aspires to be a serious painter. Ben writes, cares for, and is caught up in the misadventures and surreal stories of his younger schizophrenic brother. Laura is also a story teller as powerful and enchanting as Scheherazade. Ben struggles to survive such riches, and he and Laura endure.

Signed Confessions - Tom Walker

Guilt and a desperate need to repent drive the antiheroes in Tom Walker's dark (and often darkly funny) stories: a gullible journalist falls for the 40-year-old stripper he profiles in a magazine, a faithless husband abandons his family and joins a support group for lost souls., a merciless prosecuting attorney grapples with the suicide of his gay son, an aging misanthrope must make amends to five former victims, an egoistic naval hero is haunted by apparitions of his dead wife and a mysterious little girl. The seven tales in *Signed Confessions* measure how far guilty men will go to obtain a forgiveness no one can grant but themselves.

Body of Work - Andrei Guruianu

Throughout thirteen stories, Body of Work chronicles the physical and emotional toll of characters consumed by the all-too-human need for a connection. Their world is achingly common — beauty and regret, obsession and self-doubt, the seductive charm of loneliness. Often fragmented, whimsical, always on the verge of melancholy, the collection is a sepia-toned portrait of nostalgia — each story like an artifact of our impermanence, an embrace of all that we have lost, of all that we might lose and love again someday.

Fomite
Burlington, VT

The Housing Market - Joseph D. Reich

In Joseph Reich's most recent social and cultural, contemporary satire of suburbia entitled, "The Housing market: a comfortable place to jump off the end of the world," the author addresses the absurd, postmodern elements of what it means, or for that matter not, to try and cope and function, and survive and thrive, or live and die in the repetitive and existential, futile and self-destructive, homogenized, monochromatic landscape of a brutal and bland, collective unconscious, which can spiritually result in a gradual wasting away and erosion of the senses or conflict and crisis of a desperate, disproportionate 'situational depression,' triggering and leading the narrator to feel constantly abandoned and stranded, more concretely or proverbially spoken, "the eternal stranger," where when caught between the fight or flight psychological phenomena, naturally repels him and causes him to flee and return without him even knowing it into the wild, while by sudden circumstance and coincidence discovers it surrounds the illusory-like circumference of these selfsame Monopoly board cul-de-sacs and dead ends. Most specifically, what can happen to a solitary, thoughtful, and independent thinker when being stagnated in the triangulation of a cookie-cutter, oppressive culture of a homeowner's association; a memoir all written in critical and didactic, poetic stanzas and passages, and out of desperation, when freedom and control get taken, what he is forced to do in the illusion of 'free will and volition,' something like the derivative art of a smart and ironic and social and cultural satire.

Still Time - Michael Cocchiarale

Still Time is a collection of twenty-five short and shorter stories exploring tensions that arise in a variety of contemporary relationships: a young boy must deal with the wrath of his out-of-work father; a woman runs into a man twenty years after an awkward sexual encounter; a wife, unable to conceive, imagines her own murder, as well as the reaction of her emotionally distant husband; a soon-to-be-tenured English professor tries to come to terms with her husband's shocking return to the religion of his youth; an assembly line worker, married for thirty years, discovers the surprising secret life of his recently hospitalized wife. Whether a few hundred or a few thousand words, these and other stories in the collection depict characters at moments of deep crisis. Some feel powerless, overwhelmed—unable to do much to change the course of their lives. Others rise to the occasion and, for better or for worse, say or do the thing that might transform them for good. Even in stories with the most troubling of endings, there remains the possibility of redemption. For each of the characters, there is still time.

Raven or Crow - Joshua Amses

Marlowe has recently moved back home to Vermont after flunking his first term at a private college in the Midwest, when his sort-of girlfriend, Eleanor, goes missing. The circumstances surrounding Eleanor's disappearance stand to reveal more about Marlowe than he is willing to allow. Rather than report her missing, he resolves to find Eleanor himself. *Raven or Crow* is the story of mistakes rooted in the ambivalence of being young and without direction.

Fomite
Burlington, VT

The Good Muslim of Jackson Heights - *Jaysinh Birjépatil*
Jackson Heights in this book is a fictional locale with common features assembled from immigrant-friendly neighborhoods around the world where hardworking honest-to-goodness traders from the Indian subcontinent rub shoulders with ruthless entrepreneurs, reclusive antique-dealers, homeless nobodies, merchant-princes, lawyers, doctors, and IT specialists. But as Siraj and Shabnam, urbane newcomers fleeing religious persecution in their homeland, discover, there is no escape from the past. Weaving together the personal and the political. *The Good Muslim of Jackson Heights* is an ambiguous elegy to a utopian ideal set free from all prejudice.

Meanwell - *Janice Miller Potter*
Meanwell is a twenty-four-poem sequence in which a female servant searches for identity and meaning in the shadow of her mistress, poet Anne Bradstreet. Although Meanwell herself is a fiction, someone like her could easily have existed among Bradstreet's known but unnamed domestic servants. Through Meanwell's eyes, Bradstreet emerges as a human figure during the Great Migration of the 1600s, a period in which the Massachusetts Bay Colony was fraught with physical and political dangers. Through Meanwell, the feelings of women, silenced during the midwife Anne Hutchinson's fiery trial before the Puritan ministers, are finally acknowledged. In effect, the poems are about the making of an American rebel. Through her conflicted conscience, we witness Meanwell's transformation from a powerless English waif to a mythic American who ultimately chooses wilderness over the civilization she has experienced.

Four-Way Stop - *Sherry Olson*
If *Thank You* were the only prayer, as Meister Eckhart has suggested, it would be enough, and Sherry Olson's poetry, in her second book, *Four-Way Stop*, would be one. Radical attention, deep love, and dedication to kindness illuminate these poems and the stories she tells us, which are drawn from her own life: with family, with friends, and wherever she travels, with strangers – who to Olson, never are strangers, but kin. Even at the difficult intersections, as in the title poem, *Four-Way Stop*, Olson experiences – and offers – hope, showing us how, *completely unsupervised*, people take turns, with *kindness waving each other on*. Olson writes, knowing that (to quote Czeslaw Milosz) *What surrounds us, here and now, is not guaranteed*. To this world, with her poems, Olson brings – and teaches – attention, generosity, compassion, and appreciative joy. —Carol Henrikson

Dons of Time - *Greg Guma*
"Wherever you look...there you are." The next media breakthrough has just happened. They call it Remote Viewing and Tonio Wolfe is at the center of the storm. But the research underway at TELPORT's off-the-books lab is even more radical -- opening a window not only to remote places but completely different times. Now unsolved mysteries are colliding with cutting edge science and altered states of consciousness in a world of corporate gangsters, infamous crimes and top-secret experiments. Based on eyewitness accounts, suppressed documents and the lives of world-changers like Nikola Tesla, Annie Besant and Jack the Ripper, Dons of Time is a speculative adventure, a glimpse of an alternative future and a quantum leap to Gilded Age London at the tipping point of invention, revolution and murder.

Fomite
Burlington, VT

Screwed – Stephen Goldberg
Screwed is a collection of five plays by Stephen Goldberg, who has written over twenty-five produced plays and is co-founder of the Off Center or the Dramatic Arts in Burlington, Vermont.

Alfabestiario
AlphaBetaBestiario - Antonello Borra
Animals have always understood that mankind is not fully at home in the world. Bestiaries, hoping to teach, send out warnings. This one, of course, aims at doing the same.

The Consequence of Gesture - L.E. Smith
On a Monday evening in December of 1980, Mark David Chapman murdered John Lennon outside his apartment building in New York City. The Consequence of Gesture brings the reader along a three-day countdown to mayhem. This book inserts Chapman into the weekend plans of a group of friends sympathetic with his obsession to shatter a cultural icon and determined to perform their own iconoclastic gestures. John Lennon's life is not the only one that hangs in the balance. No one will emerge the same.

Sinfonia Bulgarica—Zdravka Evtimova
Sinfonia Bulgarica is a novel about four women in contemporary Bulgaria: a rich cold-blooded heiress, a masseuse dreaming of peace and quiet that never come, a powerful wife of the most influential man in the country, and a waitress struggling against all odds to win a victory over lies, poverty and humiliation. It is a realistic book of vice and yearning, of truthfulness and schemes, of love and desperation. The heroes are plain-spoken characters, whose action is limited by the contradictions of a society where lowness rules at many levels. The novel draws a picture of life in a country where many people believe that "Money is the most loyal friend of man". Yet the four women have an even more loyal friend: ruthlessness of life.

My Father's Keeper - Andrew Potok
The turmoil, terror and betrayal of their escape from Poland at the start of World War II lead us into this tale of hatred and forgiveness between father and son.

Fomite
Burlington, VT

Unfinished Stories of Girls —Catherine Zobal Dent
The sixteen stories in this debut collection set on the Eastern Shore of Maryland feature powerfully drawn characters with troubles and subjects such as communal guilt over a drunk-driving car accident that kills a young girl, the doomed marriage of a jewelry clerk and an undercover cop, the obsessions of a housecleaner jailed for forging her employers' signatures, the heart-breaking closeness of a family stuck in the snow. Each of Unfinished Stories of Girls' richly textured tales is embedded in the quiet and sometimes violent fields, towns, and riverbeds that are the backdrop for life in tidewater Maryland. Dent's deep love for her region shines through, but so does her melancholic thoughtfulness about its challenges and problems. The reader is invited inside the lives of characters trying to figure out the marshy world around them, when that world leaves much up to the imagination

Writing a review on Amazon, Good Reads, Shelfari, Library Thing or other social media sites for readers will help the progress of independent publishing. To submit a review, go to the book page on any of the sites and follow the links for reviews. Books from independent presses rely on reader to reader communications.

Made in the USA
Columbia, SC
16 September 2022